Holy Transfiguration Monastery

Tabor

Catholic

D0357425

95470

25-8958

The Mystery
of the Eucharist

an Ecumenical Approach

by

MAX THURIAN
Brother of Taize

Translated by Emily Chisholm

GRAND RAPIDS, MICHIGAN
WILLIAM B. EERDMANS PUBLISHING COMPANY

Copyright ©Éditions du Centurion, 1981
Originally published 1981 in French
as *Le mystère de l'eucharistie*

First published in English language 1983
by A. R. Mowbray & Co. Ltd, Oxford

This American edition published 1984 through special arrangement with
A. R. Mowbray by Wm. B. Eerdmans Publishing Company,
255 Jefferson S.E., Grand Rapids, Mich. 49503

All rights reserved
Printed in the United States of America

Library of Congress Cataloging in Publication Data

Thurian, Max.
The mystery of the Eucharist.

Translation of: Le mystère de l'Eucharistie.
1. Lord's Supper. I. Title.
BV825.2.T5313   1984   264'. 36   84-10286
ISBN 0-8028-1028-9

ACKNOWLEDGEMENTS

An extract from the First Eucharistic Prayer in the Order for Holy Communion Rite A in The Alternative Service Book 1980 is reproduced with permission.

One prayer from *Service Book and Hymnal*, copyright 1958, is reprinted by permission of Augsberg Publishing House.

Material from *The Book of Common Order*, Church of Scotland, Oxford University Press, London 1962, is reproduced by permission of the Committee on Public Worship and Aids to Devotion of the Church of Scotland.

Every effort has been made to contact the copyright holders of the epicleses. The publishers apologize for any omissions, which will be rectified in any subsequent reprint.

Contents

Introduction

Christian people eagerly await the day when all who believe in the eucharistic presence of Christ, will be able to meet regularly around the same Table. This will demand a fundamental common faith. Already the renewal of eucharistic practice in the Churches has drawn Christians much closer together. There is among many young people throughout the world a thirst for faith and for communion.

The following reflections are offered to further this development of the faith towards the unity of all Christians in that unique meal, the Lord's Supper. They touch on the problems which have arisen in the course of history, but above all they gather together the elements of common faith which have been discovered over the last few years in ecumenical dialogue.

In the light of the biblical doctrine of the memorial, the Churches are rediscovering their faith in the Eucharist as the actual and effective presence of the unique sacrifice of Jesus Christ, crucified and risen from the dead. As far as the doctrine of the real presence is concerned, the Churches are also much closer together. For all Christians, Christ, according to his promise, is made really present in his body and his blood in the celebration of the Eucharist. The rediscovery of the epiclesis, or invocation of the Holy Spirit, upon the Eucharist, gives once more to all the Churches a much deeper sense of the real presence of Christ. It is by the power of the Holy Spirit that the bread and the wine become the body and the blood of Christ. The Eucharist is the sacrament of the unique sacrifice of the cross, celebrated by the risen Christ, ever living and interceding on behalf of all humanity. It is the memorial of all that God has done for our salvation, in the incarnation, passion, resurrection and ascension of Christ. This presence of Christ, in his sacrificial memorial, is the fruit of the living word and the power of the Holy Spirit.

The Eucharist,
sacrifice of praise
and of supplication

In all religions, as far back as we can go into the known history of mankind, we discover the need to offer something to God in order to give him pleasure, or to thank him (praise and thanksgiving), in order to obtain some benefit for oneself or a blessing for others from him (supplication and intercession), or to solicit from him purification and forgiveness (expiation and propitiation). Religion, which constitutes one of the specific qualities of humankind, always implies worship given to God in the form of an offering or a sacrifice. This is closely linked to the deep psychology of man who, from his infancy, feels a need to receive and to give and is enclosed in a complex of exchange where it is vital for him to accept signs of love and to give some in return.

The Christian faith is certainly a reality transcending the religion which is present in the heart of everyman. Faith, which is a gift of sheer grace from God, has a critical function in relation to our human religious feelings. However, Christian faith, the fruit of grace, does not make a clean sweep of our religious human nature. It does not crush man the better to glorify God. It takes on our created nature to bring it to its full flowering in Christ. Faith, which operates a change in our human hearts through conversion, uses our sanctified religious nature 'to the building up of the Body of Christ, until finally all of us together shall be one in the faith and the knowledge of the Son of God and constitute that mature and perfect Man who will make actual the fullness of Christ.' (Eph. 4.12–13)

When the tradition of the Church calls the Lord's Supper or Eucharist a 'sacrifice' it is with no desire of making it one act of religious worship among other acts, not even the most noteworthy and the most spiritual. The Eucharist is a sacrifice, because it takes its place in the tradition of the sacrifices of the Old Covenant with the people of Israel, of which it is a fulfilment, in so far as it is a sacrament or actualization of the unique and perfect sacrifice of Christ on the cross. The eucharistic sacrifice therefore takes up all the sacrificial gestures of the religions of mankind along with those of the Old Testament; the Eucharist is not separated from those religious sacrifices or from the Jewish sacrifices, it fulfils them in the fullness of Christ, the perfect Man. But at the same time, it is quite different – it is the unique sacrament of the unique sacrifice of Chirst. As announced in the prophecy of Malachi, which was taken up on many occasions by the Church Fathers to indicate the Eucharist: 'I take no pleasure in the offerings of your hands; but, from the rising of the sun to its setting, my Name is great among the nations and in every place a sacrifice of incense is presented to my Name as a pure offering' (Mal. 1.10). One of the oldest references to the Eucharist, beside the Gospels, the *Didache*, edited in Syria at the end of the first century, runs as follows (XIV): 'On the Lord's Day meet together to break bread and give thanks, after you have confessed your sins also, so that your sacrifice may be pure. But any one who has a dispute with his companion will not join you before he has been reconciled, for fear that your sacrifice should be profaned. Here in fact is the word of the Lord: 'In all places and at all times let a pure sacrifice be offered to me . . .' Justin wrote in about the year 150: 'God is speaking about those sacrifices offered in every place by us the nations, the bread and the cup of the Eucharist, when he says that we glorify his name.' (*Dialogue with Tryphon*, 41.2-3) Irenaeus of Lyons alludes to this prophecy: 'The oblation which, at the Lord's command, is offered by the Church throughout the world is, in the sight of God, a pure oblation and he accepts it, not that he needs our sacrifices but because the one who offers it is glorified in his offering, when it is accepted . . . The Church alone offers with thanksgiving this pure oblation, the product of God's own creation.' (*Adv. Haer. IV*, 18,1,4)

But how does the Eucharist take its place in the continuity, and as the fulfilment of the sacrifices of the Old Covenant of the people of Israel?

THE EUCHARIST, THE NEW PASSOVER MEAL

The Lord's Supper, or Christian Eucharist, cannot be understood unless it is placed in the context of the liturgical meal, celebrated to this day every year at the Passover season. 'I have longed with all my heart to eat this Passover with you before my suffering', said Jesus to his disciples, 'for I will never eat it again until it is fulfilled in the Kingdom of God' (Luke 22, 15-16) This paschal meal will be considered as the supreme sacrifice when the sacrifices of the Temple are no more, it will be the great memorial of the deliverance of God's people.

The New Testament has left us only the essential words of those spoken by Jesus, when he celebrated the Last Supper

Holy Transfiguration Monastery
The Monks of Mt. Tabor
(Byzantine-Ukrainian Catholic)
17001 Tomki Rd., Redwood Valley, CA 95470
(707) 485-8959

with his disciples, in the framework of the Passover meal. St Paul, who received from the Lord the tradition of this celebration, recalls, as a good theologian, the commandment of Jesus which gives the Eucharist its whole meaning: 'This is my body, given for you; do this as a memorial of me . . . This cup is the new Covenant in my blood; do this whenever you drink it, as a memorial of me (*éis tèn émèn anamnèsin*).'

This word *memorial* is central in the profound significance of the Eucharist. The memorial is no mere subjective memory; it is a liturgical gesture, making actual an event in the history of salvation (the exodus of God's people or the sacrifice of Christ upon the cross) in and for the Church, and it is, at the same time, a liturgical action through which the Church presents to the Father, Christ's unique sacrifice, as her offering of thanksgiving and intercession. And so, 'do this as a memorial of me' really means, 'do this, so that my sacrifice may be present among you and my Father may remember me in your favour.' This word 'memorial' gave to the Jewish Passover meal its full significance, it made actual the deliverance of God's people; it gave to the Christian Eucharist its full significance, the actualization of the sacrifice of Christ, in the Church and in the presence of the Father.

In order to have a good understanding of the Eucharist, celebrated by Jesus in the setting of the Jewish passover meal, it is useful to understand that liturgical meal of the people of God.

The prayers of the Blessing of the Meal (*birkat ha-mazon*) were part of the Passover meal and are able to help us to understand the significance of the first Last Supper and therefore of the Eucharist itself. Here we give the prayers in the simple form which was expanded in the passover liturgy; but structure and meaning are the same. Jesus certainly used one of the forms of these prayers.

1. Blessed are you, *Lord, our God, king of the universe,*
you feed us and the whole world
with kindness, generosity and mercy.
Blessed are you Lord. You feel all creation.

2. Praise to you (*We give you thanks,*), *Lord, our God,*
for you have given us as our heritage a pleasant land,
goodly and wide, the Covenant and the Law, life and food;

for all this, we give you thanks
and we bless your Name for ever and ever.
Blessed are you, Lord, for the earth and for food.

3. Have pity *on us, Lord, our God,*
on Israel, your people, on Jerusalem, your city,
on your sanctuary, your dwelling,
on Zion, the habitation of your glory,
on your great and holy house.
Your Name has been invoked upon it;
restore the kingdom of the house of David
in its place and in our time.

(festal addition for Passover:)
Our God and God of our fathers,
may it arise, may it arrive, may it be seen
and welcomed,
may it be heard and accepted, may it be recalled
the memorial *of ourselves, the memorial*
of our fathers,
the memorial of the Messiah, the son of David, your servant,
the memorial of Jerusalem, your holy city,
the memorial of your whole people, the house of Israel,
may it be present before your face to obtain for us
liberation, prosperity, grace,
generosity, mercy, life and peace,
on this day of the festival of the Unleavened Bread.

Remember us *on this day, Lord, our God,*
and grant us prosperity,
visit us on this day and give us the blessing,
save us on this day and bestow life upon us.
By your Word of salvation and of mercy,
forgive us, grant us grace, have pity on us
and save us, for we look to you,
since you are the King full of grace and mercy.
Build up Jerusalem, the city of your holiness,
hasten it, in our time.
May you be blessed, Lord, for in your
compassion, you are building Jerusalem.

In these prayers, we find all the significance Jesus desired to give to the Eucharist of the Church, at the same time assuring her of his real presence by his Body and his Blood, the Crucified, risen again, giving himself as food.

The two first prayers beginning with 'Blessed are you . . ." and 'Praise to you . . .' refer to what biblical tradition calls the benediction or the sacrifice of praise or thanksgiving. The first style of prayer consists in recalling the wonders the Lord performed for his people, and in laying them before him. The second kind of prayer is an offering of praise and thanksgiving which arises out of the blessing in which the wonders and the gracious gifts of God are laid before him. This sacrifice of praise and thanksgiving is a kind of response to God's wonders recalled in the blessing. In Israel this spiritual sacrifice gradually replaced the material sacrifices of the Temple. The Psalms are full of this idea of the sacrifice of praise and thanksgiving. Psalm 100 is nothing but a sacrifice of praise. Psalm 26 expresses the sacrifice of praise in these words:

> *'I wash my hands in innocence*
> *and go round your altar,*
> *sounding your praises,*
> *telling all your wonders;*
> *I love the beauty of your house,*
> *the dwelling of your glory'.*

Finally, Psalm 116, part of the liturgy of the Passover meal which Jesus sang with his disciples at the Last Supper:

> *'How shall I repay to the Lord*
> *all the good he has done to me?*
> *I will raise the cup of salvation*
> *and call on the name of the Lord . . .*
> *I will offer the sacrifice of praise,*
> *and call on the name of the Lord.*
> *I will walk in the presence of the Lord*
> *in the land of the living'.*

As St Peter says, we are a royal priesthood 'to proclaim the praises of him who has called us out of darkness into his marvellous light.' (1 Peter 2.9) And the author of the Epistle to the Hebrews describes our life as Christians: 'Through Christ, let us offer a sacrifice of praise to God at all times, that is to say, the fruit of lips that confess his Name. As for generosity and community of goods, do not forget them, for it is in such sacrifices that God takes pleasure.' (Hebrews 13. 15–16; see Ps. 14, 23) The Christian life is described here as a sacrifice of generosity, a liturgy and a diaconate which are one to the glory of God.

And so, it is in the spirit of a blessing for the wonders of God and a sacrifice of praise, that Jesus celebrated the first Eucharist during the passover meal. The Church has always understood it in this way, for the oldest liturgies place at the beginning of the eucharistic prayer a solemn blessing for the wonders of creation and of redemption, which testifies that the Eucharist is a sacrifice of praise and thanksgiving:

> *'Truly it is right and good*
> *to give you thanks*
> *to offer you our thanksgiving*
> *at all times and in all places,*
> *most Holy Father,*
> *Almighty and everliving God,*
> *Creator of all things,*
> *Master of time and of history . . .'*
> (Preface, Sanctus)

The fourth eucharistic prayer of the current Roman Missal is one of the clearest examples of this sacrifice of praise and thanksgiving. But all the Churches begin their eucharistic prayer in the style of the benediction (*berakah*) and of the sacrifice of praise (*tôdah*).

The third prayer and its festal addition (*memorial*) is supplication and intercession:

> *'Have pity . . .   Remember . . .'*

The Eucharist is also supplication and intercession, based on the recall of the sacrifice of Christ. It is because Jesus gave himself to the Father and to us in the sacrifice of the cross, it is because he intercedes for us before the Father, that we, strengthened by this sacrifice and by this intercession, are able to offer the Church's eucharistic prayer as our supplication and our intercession. It is what the Bible calls the memorial: the recall before God of what he has already done for his people, so that he may grant us today all the benefits they confer. The memorial is the making actual of God's work, and it is at the same time the recall in prayer to the Father of what he has done, that he may pursue his work today.

The paschal meal is the supreme memorial, in which the people of God make the historical deliverance actual, in a liturgy, and remind God of what he once did, so that he may continue it today:

'*Our God and God of our fathers,*' says the Jewish paschal prayer, '*let it rise . . . the memorial of ourselves, the memorial of our fathers, the memorial of the Messiah . . . Remember us . . .*' How many liturgical acts of the Old Testament are called in this way 'memorial' because they are a symbolic way of saying to God: '*Remember us because of your faithfulness, manifested of old by the deliverance from slavery and by the covenant with your people!*'

In the sacrifice of the oblation or in the offering of the loaves of the food-offering, the incense is lit and the smoke rises. The text from Leviticus calls it a perfume, rising as a memorial, that is to say, recalling the one who presents the offering to remind God (Le. 2.1–3; 24.5–9). When the high priest enters the sanctuary, he wears a liturgical vestment adorned with twelve precious stones, engraved with the names of the twelve tribes of Israel. '*When he enters the sanctuary,*' says the biblical text, '*Aaron will bear on his heart the names of the sons of Israel, as a perpetual memorial before the Lord.*' (Exod. 28.29.) It is like a symbolic intercession to remind God of the twelve tribes. Numerous examples of the memorial could be given and all of them illuminate our understanding of the Eucharist. But this is not only a conception of the Old Testament. The Acts of the Apostles, for example, in the account of the conversion of Cornelius reports these words of the angel of the Lord: '*Cornelius, your prayers and your generous giving have risen as a memorial before God. And now, send men to Joppa to fetch one Simon, surnamed Peter.*' (Acts 10. 4–5, 31–32) The prayers and the charities of Cornelius have been like a call to God to remember, and he heard his call.

And so, when Christ said at the Last Supper, in the course of the paschal meal, the words, so rich in significance for Jews, '*Do this as a memorial of me,*' the apostles understood very clearly that Jesus was asking them to celebrate the Eucharist in the manner of a sacrifice of supplication and of intercession, to present to the Father the memorial of the sacrifice of the cross as a prayer full of promises for all people. And so it is that a great exegete could translate the words of Christ at the Last Supper, 'Do this so that the Father remembers me.' (J. Jeremias) To take up the wording of the Jewish Passover liturgy, this annotation on the words of Jesus could be made: *'Our Lord and God of our fathers, let the memorial of the Messiah, the son of your servant David, the memorial of his sacrifice, rise before your face . . . Remember us!'*

The Jewish Passover liturgy, in the course of which Jesus celebrated the Last Supper, gives us to understand that the Eucharist is a blessing for the marvels of God, a sacrifice of praise and thanksgiving, a memorial, that is to say an actualization of the passion, the resurrection and the intercession of Christ, a memorial lifted up before the Father as the offering of the prayer of the Church, reminding God of all the needs of men: 'Remember, Lord, your Church and all for whom we present the sacrifice.' As a very beautiful prayer of the Catholic liturgy expresses it: *'Lord, look with favour on your Church's offering, and see the Victim whose death has reconciled us to yourself.'* (Eucharistic Prayer III)

These various stages in the prayer of the Jewish Passover meal have given its structure to Christian eucharistic prayer; beginning with the blessing for the marvels of God and the sacrifice and praise to the Father (*berakah - tôdah:* preface - sanctus), it continues with the memorial of the salvation events in Christ, presented to the Father to remind him of this people (*anamnesis* - sacrificial memorial), concluding with supplication and intercession that the Father may grant a new outpouring of the Holy Spirit on the Church, and that he may hear her in her prayers for all whom she remembers. 'Remember, Lord . . .' (*epiclesis* – mementos).

THE EUCHARISTIC SACRIFICE

If we return to what the Jewish liturgy of the Passover meal provides for the understanding of the Eucharist in depth, we might offer the following summary to explain why it can be said that the Eucharist is a sacrifice:

1. it is a *sacrifice of praise and thanksgiving* recalling the mar-

vels wrought by God in the order of creation and the order of redemption;

2. it is the *sacrament of the unique sacrifice* of Christ: the sacramental presence of the sacrifice of the cross;
3. it is the *liturgical presentation* of the sacrifice of the Son by the Church to the Father, to remind him of this people and to grant them the blessings afforded by that unique sacrifice;
4. it is *participation in the Son's intercession* with the Father for the gift of salvation to all people and for the coming of the Kingdom of God.

1. *The Eucharist, as a sacrifice of praise and of thanksgiving*

If there is one theme on which all Christian tradition agrees, it is surely this: the Eucharist is a sacrifice of praise and thanksgiving. As early as the middle of the second century, St Justin was writing: 'The offering of flour (in Jewish worship), the offering prescribed for those who have been cleansed from leprosy, was a figure of the bread of the Eucharist which Jesus Christ our Lord prescribed for us to celebrate as a memorial of the passion he suffered for all humanity, to purify their hearts of all perversity; Jesus prescribed that we should celebrate the Eucharist in order also to thank God for creating the world with all that it contains, for our use, and for delivering us from the sin in which we were born . . .' (*Dialogue with Tryphon*, 41.1.)

The Eucharist is not only a sacrament relating to the liberation of all people, accomplished by Christ on the cross, it is also a sacrifice of praise, *thanksgiving for the work of creation*. As St Irenaeus of Lyons also said at a later date: 'In thanksgiving to her Creator the Church offers this pure oblation which is a product of his own creation.' (*Adv. Haer*, IV, 18.4) It is very important for us to see reconciled in the Eucharist the order of creation and the order of redemption. Too often, in a puritanical spirit, Christians, concerned only for their salvation and cleansing from sins, made of the Eucharist a sad, pious remembrance of the passion of Christ, as a cure for sin. The Fathers of the Church remind us that present also in the Eucharist is the whole creation and the world God loves, and that there we can offer the sacrifice of praise and of thanksgiving for all good and beautiful things created by God in the world and in human beings. The Church today needs to remember this cosmic, ecological, positive and optimistic vision of the Eucharist and to celebrate in a liturgy expressing the joy of heaven on earth and our expectation of the feast in the Kingdom of Heaven.

At this point I cannot forbear to quote a beautiful passage from Calvin, whom history has so often falsely portrayed as austere and puritanical. This is what he wrote about the Lord's Supper as a sacrifice of praise:

'(This kind of sacrifice is) in the Supper of our Lord, in which, when we proclaim and remember his death and give thanks, we do nothing else but offer a sacrifice of praise. Because of this sacrificial office, all of us Christians are called a royal priesthood (1 Peter, 2.9), since through Jesus Christ we offer a sacrifice of praise to God, that is to say the fruit of lips that confess his name. . . For we cannot appear before God with our gifts and presents without an intercessor. And this Mediator is Jesus Christ, interceding for us, by whom we offer ourselves and all that is ours to our Father. He is our high priest, who has entered into the Sanctuary of heaven. He opens it to us and gives us access. He is our altar; on him we place our offerings; in him we dare all that we dare. In short, it is he who has made us kings and priests for the Father.'
(*Inst. Chrét.* IV, XVIII. 17.)

2. *The Eucharist as a sacrament of the sacrifice*

Without diminishing in any way the unique character of the cross, the forgiveness, reconciliation and liberation achieved by the unique sacrifice of Christ, the Eucharist is the sacrament, or the presence of the unique sacrifice of Christ who continues today his work of saving all mankind. The Eucharist is the cross present in the Church, extending to all people in space, in time and in depth, the unique and perfect work of Christ. In the Eucharist, the Church meets Christ who communicates to each believer the fruits of the sacrifice of the cross and the present intercession of the Saviour.

The sacramental presence of the sacrifice of the cross is accomplished by the power of the Holy Spirit and of the Word.

21

No action of the Church is conceived outside the work of the Holy Spirit and no sacramental liturgy can omit to mention it. The real presence of Christ and of his sacrifice in the Eucharist is a fruit of his Word that is full of promise: *'This is my body . . . This cup is the new Covenant in my blood . . .'*, but this word is not a magic formula which would operate simply by being spoken. It is the Holy Spirit which gives life to these words and makes them actual in the sacrament celebrated by the Church. Without the activity of the Spirit in the Eucharist this text would remain a dead letter. A true celebration of the eucharistic sacrifice is a celebration in the Holy Spirit with the Word of Christ. This means that a eucharistic liturgy will include Christ's words of the institution of the Last Supper and an invocation to the Holy Spirit. These together accomplish the mystery of the living presence of Christ and of his sacrifice.

The Holy Spirit makes Christ crucified and risen from the dead to be really present for us in the eucharistic meal, fulfilling the promise contained in the words of the institution of the Last Supper. The Holy Spirit's role in the Eucharist is to make actual and to vitalize the historical words of Christ. It is not a matter of spiritualizing the eucharistic presence of Christ, but of affirming an indissoluble union between the Son and the Spirit. This union shows that the Eucharist is not a magical automatic action, but a prayer addressed to the Father emphasizing the total dependence of the Church upon him. Certain of being heard, because of the promise of Jesus in the words of the institution, the Church asks the Father for the Holy Spirit so that he will accomplish the eucharistic event: the real presence of Christ crucified and risen, giving his life for humankind. The words of the institution, Christ's promise, and the epiclesis, the invocation of the Spirit, are therefore in close relationship in the liturgy.

The Catholic Church has realized the relationship between the Spirit and the presence of the sacrifice of Christ in the Eucharist, because she has restored the epiclesis into her liturgy after the Second Vatican Council: *'We implore you to consecrate yourself the offerings which we bring. Sanctify them by your Spirit, so that they become the body and the blood of your Son, Jesus Christ, our Lord, who told us to celebrate this mystery. . .'*

And so it is in virtue of the living word of Christ and by the power of the Holy Spirit that the Eucharist becomes the sacrament or the presence of the unique sacrifice of Christ crucified and risen again, our high priest and intercessor before the face of the Father.

3. *The Eucharist, the presentation of the sacrifice*

The Eucharist is the liturgical presentation by the Church of the sacrifice to the Father. This liturgical presentation is the action which recalls to God the Father the unique sacrifice of his Son, which is eternally actual, and implores him by this sacrifice to grant mercies and blessings to his people.

As she proclaims the sacrifice of Christ, the Church accomplishes on the altar the setting forth of the sacrifice of the Son before the Father, giving him thanks and beseeching him to grant his grace. Thus, in this gesture of showing forth the cross, the Church participates in the offering of the Lamb sacrificed, as it were, on the heavenly altar, and in the intercession presented by the Son before the Father's face.

The French Reformation theologians of the seventeenth century were to insist on the memorial and sacrificial aspect in the Lord's Supper. Pastor Pierre du Moulin of Paris in his famous book *Le bouclier de la foi* (1635) expressed it as follows: 'There are particular reasons why the Last Supper can be termed "sacrifice" ':

(a) This sacrament was instituted to proclaim the Lord's death till he comes; and so the Lord's Supper may be called sacrifice because it represents the sacrifice of the Lord's death. . .
(b) It can be said that in the Last Supper we offer Jesus Christ to God, in that we pray God to receive for us the sacrifice of his death.
(c) The Lord's Supper is a eucharistic sacrifice, that is to say a sacrifice of thanksgiving for God's blessings . . .' (p. 629 ff.)

Another seventeenth century theologian, Jacques Basnage (1653–1723), sums up this idea of the presentation to the Father of the unique sacrifice of the Son as intercession from the Church in a sentence, too cut and dried perhaps, but having the advantage of clarity: 'No new sacrifice is being made (in the Eucharist), but a commemoration of the Son of God's sacrifice, presented to the Father under the symbols of the bread and the wine, does not fail to move him to grant us the fruits of the real sacrifice, that of the cross.' (*Histoire de l'Eglise* . . ., Rotterdam 1699, p. 995)

4. The Eucharist, participation in the intercession of the Risen Lord

When the Church celebrates the Eucharist, she enters once more into intimacy with her Lord and gives continually renewed expression to his unique and eternal intercessions.

The Eucharist is one of the essential forms of the life of Christ as priest and intercessor in the Church. It is for the Church to introduce, or rather to allow to be introduced into her liturgy, the unique and eternal intercession of Christ crucified and risen again. Historically he lived this intercession once and for all on the cross, and he continues to live it eternally in glory and sacramentally in his Body, which is the Church. The Church manifests and focuses the redemptive intercession of the Son of God by means of the Eucharist through which his passion and his resurrection are made visible and actual.

In a very beautiful passage, Luther showed how Christ's intercession and the offering of the Church are closely united in the Eucharist: 'We do not offer Christ, but it is Christ who offers us (to God). In this way it is legitimate, indeed useful, to call the ceremony a sacrifice, not just in itself as such, but because in it we offer ourselves in sacrifice with Christ. In other words, we entrust ourselves to Christ, believing firmly in his covenant and we present ourselves before God with our prayer, praise and sacrifice, only in the name of Christ, and through him . . . never doubting that he is our Priest in heaven face to face with God. Christ welcomes us, he presents us (to God), us, our prayers and our praises; he also offers himself in heaven for us . . . He offers himself for us in heaven, and offers us with himself.' (1520, Weimar Edition VI, 369.)

The Church of Scotland's liturgy has given very beautiful expression to the union in Christ's intercession:

'Wherefore, having in remembrance the work and passion of our Saviour Christ, and pleading His eternal sacrifice, we Thy servants do set forth this memorial, which He hath commanded us to make;

24

and we most humbly beseech Thee to send down Thy Holy Spirit to sanctify both us and these Thine own gifts of bread and wine which we set before Thee, that the bread which we break may be the Communion of the body of Christ, and the cup of blessing which we bless the Communion of the blood of Christ; that we, receiving them, may by faith be made partakers of His body and blood, with all His benefits, to our spiritual nourishment and growth in grace, and to the glory of Thy most holy name' (Book of Common Order, Edinburgh 1962.)

This presentation of the memorial in communion with the intercession of Christ, itself based on the sacrifice of the cross, is a most accurate expression of the eucharistic sacrifice. All the more so as this memorial is defined a moment later as a sacrifice of thanksgiving and intercession, closely linked with the communion:

'And here we offer and present unto Thee ourselves, our souls and bodies, to be a reasonable, holy, and living sacrifice; and we beseech Thee mercifully to accept this our sacrifice of praise and thanksgiving, as, in fellowship with all the faithful in heaven and on earth, we pray Thee to fulfil in us, and in all men, the purpose of Thy redeeming love; through Jesus Christ our Lord, by whom, and with whom, in the unity of the Holy Spirit, all honour and glory be unto Thee, O Father Almighty, world without end. Amen.'

The eucharistic sacrifice implores God to extend salvation to all people, to accomplish the sanctification of believers until the return of Christ, and to grant liberation to all who do not know him as yet.

After all, if Christ has accomplished all that is necessary for the salvation of all people, if objective redemption and reconciliation are accomplished in fact on the cross, the Church, the Body of Christ, still has to be the instrument by which the graces of salvation are extended to each and to all.

Through the Eucharist, seen as a sacrifice of intercession, the Church unites with the intercession of Christ, which is founded on his sacrifice on the cross, beseeching the Father for all, for the forgiveness of their sins, for their liberation and their happiness, and she prays for the glorious manifestation of the Kingdom.

In communion with the intercession of Christ, and with his sacrifice on the cross, the Church, in presenting to the Father the memorial of this sacrifice of praise and supplication, offers herself, and each believer offers himself in an act of adoration and consecration. As Luther wrote: '. . . we present ourselves before God with our prayer, praise and sacrifice only in the name of Christ, and through him . . . He offers himself for us in heaven, and offers us with himself.' And Calvin gave this remarkable image: Jesus Christ in the heavenly sanctuary 'is our altar on which we lay our oblations; in him we dare all that we dare'.

By herself, the Church can offer or present nothing but her wretchedness to God, but in Christ she can offer a true sacrifice of thanksgiving and of intercession, for she is able to present the sacrifice of the cross to the Father as she unites in the intercession of the Son; she presents the Body of Christ and she presents herself as the Body of Christ: that is her true praise, her efficacious prayer, and the sacrifice possible for her because it is the very sacrifice of Christ, and he himself offers and presents it.

THE EUCHARIST, THE OFFERING OF CREATION

On reading the Fathers and the liturgies of the early Church, the presence of creation in the Eucharist and in liturgy in general, cannot fail to impress us. St Irenaeus of Lyons (*Adversus Haereses* IV, 17–18), points out that the liturgy begins with an oblation of the first fruits of God's own creatures. The bread and the wine come from the creation and are offered to the Creator in gratitude for his material gifts, that he may consecrate them by his Word and make of them the Body and the Blood of Christ, the only perfect sacrifice. The offertory is an important time in the celebration of the Eucharist: it proves that the Church has kept up the oblation of the first fruits of the earth and that this oblation forms the link between the order of creation and the order of redemption, which will be shown forth in the memorial sacrifice. Those theologians and liturgists who play down the offertory in order to place the emphasis wholly on the memorial sacrifice of Christ, separate creation from redemption and detach the Eucharist from the world of creation and of humankind, making it into a purely spiritual means of grace. There is a serious danger here which might detract from the universality of the eucharistic mystery.

The new words for the offertory in the Catholic liturgy are so rich in meaning. The bread is *the fruit of the earth,* the wine *the fruit of the vine;* both are the fruits of *human labour;* we present them to the God of the universe that *they may become the bread of life* and the *wine of the eternal Kingdom,* the Body and the Blood of Christ. The liturgy indicates here a double transformation: the wheat and the vine have been acted upon by man to become bread and wine; man offers them to the Creator, so that God may act upon them by his Spirit to make them the Body and the Blood of Christ. This double transformation of creation is indicated in the offering and in the consecration.

St Hyppolytus of Rome, at the beginning of the third century also speaks often about the oblation of the first fruits of the creation (*Apostolic Tradition*). Bread and wine are offered, but also milk and honey, water, oil, olives, fruit and flowers . . . The liturgy proclaims the marvels of creation and the marvels of redemption at one and the same time.

We would need to recover fully this sense of the oblation of creation in the Eucharist to show convincingly that the liturgy is not separate from man, it assumes his whole nature: he can offer at the same time the gifts of creation and the supreme gift of the Body and the Blood of Christ.

The Church's offertory, in which she brings to the altar the material and spiritual goods of the faithful, is in a way an act of offering which includes a crisis. When the Church has gathered all together to present it to God, she realizes her poverty; she can do nothing now but lay her wretchedness in the hands of Christ, who takes it up into his own sacrifice, presented in intercession and makes it into an act of true praise, efficacious prayer and valid sacrifice, 'through him, with him and in him'.

The Eucharist is the sacrament of the unique sacrifice of Christ, who ever lives to intercede for all the human race. It is the memorial of all that God has done for the salvation of the world. What God planned to accomplish in the incarnation, life, death, resurrection and ascension of Christ, he will not do a second time; those events are unique, they can neither be repeated nor prolonged. But, in the memorial of the Eucharist, they become active, here and now, for all for whom the Church offers her intercessions, in communion with Christ the High Priest and Intercessor.

The Eucharist,
real and living
presence of Christ

Christ fulfils in many ways his promise to be with his own for ever until the end of the world. He is present whenever two or three are met together in his name; he is present in the reading and proclamation of the Word of God; he is present in baptism; he is present in the poor and in those who suffer . . . But the mode of the presence of Christ in the Eucharist is unique. Jesus spoke these words over the bread and the wine of the Last Supper: *'This is my body, given for you; do this in remembrance of me . . . This cup is the new Covenant in my blood; do this in remembrance of me. . .'* (1 Cor. 11.24–25) The Church has always given a realistic meaning to these words. What Christ said is the truth and is fulfilled every time the Eucharist is celebrated. Under the outward signs of bread and wine, the profound reality is the whole being of Christ, who comes to us to feed us and transform our whole being. The Church confesses the real, living and active presence of Christ in the Eucharist. It is Christ who binds himself, by his Word and the power of the Holy Spirit, to the eucharistic elements, the signs that his presence is given.

As Calvin wrote: 'If the representation God makes to us in the Supper is true, the inward substance of the Sacrament is conjoined with the visible signs: and as the bread is distributed into our hands, the Body of Christ is communicated to us, so that we are made participants of it . . . We all confess then, with one voice' he continues, 'that receiving the Sacrament in Faith, according to the Lord's ordinance, we are truly made participants in the very substance of the body and blood of

Jesus Christ.' (*Petit traité de la sainte cène*, pp. 112, 141.) And the Augsburg Confession affirms very plainly for the Churches of Lutheran tradition: 'As to the Lord's Supper, we teach that the very Body and the very Blood of Christ are truly present in the Supper in the form of bread and wine and it is thus that they are shared and received.' (no. X.)

THE DIFFERENT CONCEPTIONS OF THE REAL PRESENCE

In the course of the Church's tradition different conceptions of the presence of Christ in the Eucharist appeared. Some may seem to be complementary, others contradictory. They all represent an effort of human intelligence to understand an unfathomable mystery of the faith, able to be worshipped rather than comprehended. These different attempts, in so far as they originate in an approach to the Word of God, in prayer and in the eucharistic life itself are most worthy of respect, even if their results are sometimes precarious. Speaking of the presence of Christ, real and alive in the Eucharist, it is really appropriate to use St Paul's exclamation as he gave expression to another mystery: 'O the depth of the riches, of the wisdom and the knowledge of God! How unfathomable his judgements and unsearchable his ways! Who indeed has known the thinking of the Lord? Or who has been his counsellor? Or who gave first to him and deserves to be repaid? For everything is from him, through him and for him. To him be glory for ever and ever. Amen'. (Rom. 11.33–36.) Echoing this confession of the mystery of God, a saintly bishop, for whom the Eucharist was indeed at the heart of life, faith and theology, said to me one day in the course of dialogue on the Real Presence: 'The mystery of the eucharistic presence of Christ is not to be manipulated, but worshipped!'

The different conceptions of the real presence do not exclude each other (when they are not contradictory); they can complement and correct each other where one may be too one-sided. It can be said, for example, that the Oriental Churches are mostly metabolist, that is to say that they emphasize chiefly the change of the elements into the Body and Blood of Christ, while the Western Churches, without denying the change, (the doctrine of transubstantiation is evidence of that), adhere rather to the idea of the sacrament-sign which at the same time manifests and conceals the presence of Christ. We will now characterize the different positions, bringing out in each one its strong accentuation of one aspect of the understanding of the mystery.

1. *The literalist conception*

The first Christians received the words of Jesus (*'This is my body . . . This is my blood . . .'*) as transmitted by the tradition of the Gospels and the Apostle Paul. They did not attempt to find a rational explanation. The literal words or texts were sufficient for them to believe in the real presence of Christ. Several of the Fathers of the Church bear witness to this literalist conception of the presence of Christ in the Eucharist.

St Ignatius of Antioch asserts that 'the Eucharist is the flesh of our Saviour Jesus Christ, who suffered for our sins and who by the Father in his goodness, was raised from the dead.' (Smyrn. VII. 1.)

St Justin, about the year 150, is just as categorical:

'We do not receive the Eucharist as ordinary bread or as an ordinary drink. But just as our Saviour Jesus Christ was made flesh by the Word of God and took flesh and blood for our salvation, in the same way, we have learned, that by the words of prayer received from him, the eucharistic food is the flesh and blood of Jesus incarnate, food which is assimilated and nourishes our flesh and our blood' (*1 Apol. 66.2.*)

St Iraeneus of Lyons, also in the second century, writes in reply to the docetists who deny the reality of Christ's humanity:

'Just as the bread which comes from the earth, is no longer ordinary bread after the invocation of God, but the Eucharist, constituted of two things, one earthly and the other heavenly, so our bodies which participate in the Eucharist are no longer corruptible, since they have the hope of the resurrection.' (*Adv. Haer*, 18.5.)

St Cyprian of Carthage is just as positive and literalist when he writes of unrepentant apostates who request communion, and declares: 'They do violence to his Body and his Blood and they sin more seriously against the Lord with their hands and their mouths than when they denied him.' (*De Laps.* 16.)

It is this same literalist conception which Martin Luther sustains when he opposes Zwingli and those he calls visionaries, who make of the Eucharist a mere symbol of the body and blood of Christ. In his treatise *Of the Lord's Supper*, in 1528, Luther writes: 'We must affirm purely and simply! This is my body, taking the words as they are . . . As for the text of the Last Supper, we want to have one only, and that simple, certain and sure in all its words, syllables and letters.' (Ed. of Weimer XXVI. 265.) In fidelity to the literal text, Luther always refused any explanation which aimed at a rational understanding of the real presence, as well as the explanation of the 'visionaries' who reduce the Supper to a symbol, as that of the 'scholastics' who distinguish between the substance of the Body of Christ and the accidents or appearances of the bread. For him, there is only the mystery, stated purely and simply by the very words of Christ.

Already in 1522, he was writing to Paul Speratus, a priest, author of spiritual songs: 'What good is served by entangling people in subtleties, when they can be directed by a sound and certain faith which believes that under the species of bread there lies the body of him who is true God and true man . . .? Faith desires to know nothing more than this: under the species of bread there is the body of Christ and under the species of wine there is the blood of Christ who lives and reigns. Let the believer persevere in this simplicity, despising idle questions.' (W. 11 560.)

2. *The metabolist conception*

The literalist conception which would like to be content with the words of Christ, very soon calls forth the metabolist conception, according to which a change (*métabolè*) takes place during the celebration of the Eucharist. If Christ spoke the truth, the bread and the wine of the Eucharist are no longer ordinary food and drink, they are changed, they become the Body and Blood of Christ, the real and living presence of Christ crucified and risen from the dead. This change is brought about by action combined with the Word of the Lord,

'*This is my body . . . This is my blood*', and by the outpouring of the Holy Spirit invoked upon the Eucharist, the epiclesis. The Eastern liturgies initiated a considerable development of this invocation of the Spirit upon the eucharistic meal, upon the bread and the wine and also upon the liturgical assembly. The influence of these liturgies upon the catecheses of the Fathers of the Church was to influence the development of eucharistic doctrine in the direction of a changing of the bread and the wine into the Body and Blood of Christ. One of the eucharistic prayers which is most explicit in the metabolist sense is the *anaphora* of St James, from the liturgical family of Antioch in the fourth century. The epiclesis, or invocation of the Holy Spirit is in these words:

'*Have pity on us, God, Father almighty.*
Have pity on us, God, our Saviour.
Have pity on us, God, according to your great mercy
and send on us and upon these holy gifts set before you
your most holy Spirit, the Lord and Giver of life;
he is seated with you, God and Father and with your only Son;
he reigns, consubstantial and coeternal;
he spoke in the Law, the Prophets and the New Testament;
he descended in the form of a dove on our Lord
Jesus Christ at the Jordan River
and he rested upon him;
he descended upon the holy apostles
in the form of tongues of fire
in the Upper Room of the sacred and glorious city of Zion,
on the day of holy Pentecost.
Send him, your most holy Spirit, Lord,
upon us and upon these holy gifts before you,
that, by his holy good and glorious coming,
he may sanctify this bread and make it the sacred body of Christ
(Amen),
may sanctify this cup and make it the precious blood of Christ
(Amen),
and may they become for all who
participate the remission of sins
and eternal life . . .'

A text attributed to St Athanasius of Alexandria turns a spotlight on this conception of the conversion of the bread and the wine which was to be that of the majority of the Church Fathers of the fourth century: 'You will see the Levites bringing loaves and cups of wine and placing them on the table. For as long as the prayers and invocations have not been said, they are only bread and a cup.

But after the great and wonderful prayers have been said, the bread becomes the body and the cup the blood of our Lord Jesus Christ . . . When the great prayers and the holy supplications are raised to God, the Word descends upon the bread and on the cup and the bread becomes his body . . .' (PG 26.1325.)

For the Fathers the transformation takes place during the eucharistic prayer as a whole which includes in any case the words of Jesus at the institution of the Last Supper and an invocation of the Holy Spirit or of the Word (epiclesis). It is the Holy Spirit or the Word (Logos) which, together with the words of Jesus, accomplishes this mysterious transformation of the bread and of the wine into the body and the blood of Christ.

St Cyril of Jerusalem, in the *Mystagogical Catecheses* attributed to him, alludes to the epiclesis in the liturgy:

'We implore God who loves mankind to send the Holy Spirit upon these gifts before him, and make the bread the body and the wine the blood of Christ; for all that is touched by the Holy Spirit becomes sanctified and transformed.' (*Myst. Cat.* V.7.)

Theodore of Mopsuestia emphasizes the link between the words of Jesus and the invocation of the Spirit in the transformation of the bread and wine of the Eucharist:

'When the priest declares that they (the bread and the wine) are the body and the blood of Christ, he makes it plain that that is what they have become by the descent of the Holy Spirit.' (*Hom. Catech.* 16.12.)

And, to affirm the reality of the transformation, he also says:

'The Lord did not say: This is the symbol of my body, this is the symbol of my blood, but: This is my body, this is my blood, teaching us that we are not to consider the nature of what is offered, but that by the intervention of the thanksgiving (the eucharistic prayer), there is transformation into body and blood.' (*In Mat. Hom.*, PG 66, 714.)

St Ambrose of Milan was to influence the Western Church by also insisting on the metabolist conception. He was to view the transformation of the bread and the wine as brought about chiefly by the words of the institution of the Lord's Supper spoken by Jesus, while the Eastern Fathers added as well the action of the Holy Spirit or the Logos. He writes plainly: 'You are perhaps saying: It is ordinary bread, isn't it? This bread is bread before the sacramental words; as soon as the consecration takes place, the bread changes into the flesh of Christ. Then let's prove it. How can what is bread be the body of Christ? By what words is the consecration effected and who spoke these words? The Lord Jesus . . . What are these words of Christ? The ones by which everything was made. The Lord gave the word and the heavens were made. The Lord gave the word, and the earth was made. The Lord gave the word and the seas were made. The Lord gave the word and all creatures were created. You see then how effective is the word of Christ. If then there is in the word of the Lord Jesus such great power that what was not began to be, how much more effective is his word to make what was exist now and be changed into something else.' (*De Sacr.* IV.14–15.)

And so the idea of the changing (*métabolè*) of bread and wine into the body and blood of Christ was to be the most widespread idea in the Church of the fourth century, and onwards, to express the real and living presence of the Lord in the Eucharist.

3. *The sacramental conception*

Affirming the change of bread and wine into the body and blood of Christ does not hinder the Fathers of the Church from speaking of the Eucharist as of a sacrament, a sign or a figure. Indeed, if the profound reality of the Eucharist has become Christ, thanks to a change accomplished by the Holy Spirit and the words of Jesus, the external appearance, the nature of bread and wine subsist for our human senses and can be called figure, sign or sacrament, under which is hidden the mysterious reality of the body and of the blood and the Lord.

St Cyril of Jerusalem, whom we have seen so categorical as far as the effectiveness of the epiclesis of the Spirit in transforming the bread and the wine is concerned, does not hesitate to use the term figure also to designate the bread and the wine: 'Once, of his own volition, Jesus changed water into wine at Cana of Galilee, and should he not be worthy of our belief when he changes wine into blood? Called to a celebration of physical marriage, he accomplishes this marvellous miracle, and, when he gives the present of the enjoyment of his body and his blood to the bridegroom's companions, will we not acknowledge it much more? It is therefore with absolute assurance that we participate in some manner in the body and the blood of Christ. For under the figure of bread the body is given to you and under the figure of wine the blood is given to you, that, when you have participated in the body and in the blood of Christ, you may become one body and one blood with Christ. And so we become 'bearers of Christ', as his body and his blood spread through our members. In this way, according to the Blessed Peter, we become 'associates of the divine nature'. (*Myst. Cat.* IV.2–3.)

Tertullian was already speaking of the eucharistic bread as a figure of the body of Christ and saying that 'in the bread Christ represents his true body.' (*Adv. Marc.* 3.19; 1.14.) The verb 'represent' must here be taken in the strong meaning of 'making present.' When Calvin, later, used this same term it was also in this strong sense:

'The communication we have with the body and the blood of the Lord Jesus is a spiritual mystery, impossible to see with the human eye or understand with the human mind. It is therefore figured to us by visible signs as our infirmity requires, but, nevertheless, not as a mere figure, but united with its truth and substance. The bread is therefore rightly called body, since not only does the bread represent the body to us, it also presents it . . . the name of the body of Jesus is transferred to the bread because it is the sacrament and figure of it.' (*Petit traité de la sainte cène*, p. 111.)

The *Apostolic Constitutions* said of the elements of the Eucharist that they are 'the antitypes of the precious body and blood of Christ': the death of Christ is recalled as a memorial 'thanks to the symbols of his body and his blood.' (*Apost. Const.* 5, 14, 7; 6, 23, 5; 7, 25, 4.) We have seen that Cyril of Jerusalem spoke of the figure (type) of bread which gives the body of Christ. In the eucharistic liturgy reported by St Ambrose, the offering is 'the figure' (*figura*) of the body and the blood of our Lord Jesus Christ' (*De Sacr.* IV 21.)

St Augustine, in his deep concern as a pastor to maintain

believers in a balanced faith, placed great emphasis upon the idea of sacrament. He wanted to maintain at its full strength belief in the presence of Christ in the eucharistic celebration while at the same time excluding the idea of carnal mastication of the physical flesh of Christ. Rather than carnal presence he affirms real participation in the resurrection of Christ by means of the sacrament (*in sacramento*). By reason of the mystery of the ascension, we are sharing in the sacrament of the flesh of the resurrection Christ. 'You are eternal life itself, and you give in your flesh and your blood nothing else than what you are.' (*Tract.* 27.1–6, 11–12, *In Joh. Ev.* 6.60–63, of 414.)

This sacramental conception of the Eucharist does not lessen conviction of the real and living presence of Christ, it attempts to understand the fact that, by the words of Jesus and the power of the Spirit, the true body and the true blood of Christ are given to us, but that our senses, nevertheless continue to perceive bread and wine; these, then are the sacrament (the sign, symbol, type antitype, figure) of the body and blood of Christ whom they represent and present in reality.

Calvin has formulated and resumed most felicitously the sense of this sacramental conception:

'If God can neither deceive nor lie, it follows that he achieves all that he says. Therefore we must truly receive in the Supper the body and the blood of Jesus Christ as the Lord represents the communion of one and the other in it . . . We must therefore confess that, if the representation which God makes to us in the Supper is true, the inner substance of the Sacrament is conjoined with the visible signs; and as the bread is placed in our hands, the body of Christ is communicated to us, so that we are made participants.' (*Petit traité de la sainte cène*, p. 112.)

4. *The realistic conception*

The balance between the metabolist conception and the sacramental conception assured by the liturgies produced in the course of the first four centuries of the Church was maintained for several centuries. The catecheses of the Fathers were agreed in affirming the reality of the living presence of Christ in the Eucharist, and the necessary distinction between the body and the blood of the Lord and the figures or signs of the bread and the wine which contained the mystery, both manifested and concealed it. Reality and sacrament were not mutually exclusive in patristic thought and in the liturgy of the Eucharist. Quite the contrary, the sacrament was the bearer of the reality without being completely identified with it; the reality was signified by the sacrament, just as a person is revealed in a face.

Two crises happened in the ninth and eleventh centuries and upset this balance, preparing the drawing-up of positions by the Western Church. First, two monks, Paschasius Radbertus, abbot of Corbie (†865), and Ratramneus (†875) took opposite viewpoints in their doctrine on the Eucharist.

For the first of them, either the Eucharist gives us the risen Christ or it is nothing: 'Spiritually an organic part of our own body, the flesh of Christ is capable of transforming us so that Christ's substance exists in our flesh as evidently as he has taken our substance into his divinity.' (*De Corp. et Sang. Dom.* XIX.15.) And, in a letter to the monk, Frudegard, Paschasius Radbertus clearly asserts the realism of the presence of Christ in the Eucharist: 'Jesus affirms: whoever does not eat this flesh and drink this wine has no life in him. And so this sacrament which confers life, possesses what it gives to all who receive it as they ought. If life is in this sacrament, this sacrament is the flesh of him who is truly alive, it is the blood in which there is in all truth the life which lasts for ever and ever.' (PL 120. 1351ff). For Paschasius Radbertus, the flesh of Christ has become Eucharist, by the resurrection, and this sacrament which is the flesh of him who is truly alive communicates to us the life of the Risen Christ.

Ratramnus, for his part, was shocked by this realism, for the body of the Christ of history is glorified in heaven; the Eucharist is merely a sacramental body, a figure, which is, by faith, a spiritual nourishment for us.

This opposition between reality and sacrament, which was unknown to the early Church, was to trouble subsequent theology. The positions of Ratramnus turned up once more in Zwingli and his disciples in the sixteenth century. For this theological line, the Eucharist is merely a figure of the body of Christ because Jesus is risen and has been raised into glory. According to the realistic conception of Paschasius Radbertus, which was to be adopted by the Western Church, a true

Eucharist must give the flesh of the Risen Christ who is eternal life.

Berengar of Tours (†1088) experienced the same difficulties as Ratramnus as far as the reality of the body of Christ in the Eucharist is concerned (since he is glorified in heaven) and he signed a strange formulation imposed by the Synod of Rome in 1059, which opposed the sacramental conception against the reality of the presence of Christ, an opposition entirely foreign to patristic and liturgical tradition, as we have already seen; this is the formulation: 'After the consecration, the bread and the wine are not only the sacrament, but also the true body and blood of Christ and tangibly, not only sacramentally, but in truth handled by the hands of the priests, broken and crushed by the teeth of the faithful.' As he had retracted, Berengar had to sign another oath at the Synod of Rome in 1079: 'I Berengar, believe in my heart and confess with my lips that the bread and the wine which are placed on the altar, are, by the mystery of the holy prayer and the words of our Redeemer, transformed in substance into the very flesh – his own life-giving flesh – and into the blood of Jesus Christ, our Lord, and that, after the consecration, they are the true body of Christ, who was born of the Virgin, hung upon the cross, was offered up for the salvation of the world, and is seated at the right hand of the Father, and the actual blood of Christ which flowed from his side; this, not only by sign and virtue of a sacrament, but in their own nature and in their actual substance . . .' (*Denz. En. Symb.* 355.)

Here, once again, there is an opposition between the sacramental sign and the actual reality; this is because, in the polemics, the sacramental sign became the mere figure of a distant reality, Christ in glory.

Luther, who had to battle against the same minimalist conception of the sacramental sign in Zwingli and the 'visionaries,' fully subscribed to Berengar's first oath (under Pope Nicholas II, in 1059). To drive home his confirmed belief in the real presence, Luther uses as always an exaggerated expression, which evokes a too carnal conception of the Eucharist for which St Augustine would certainly have felt repugnance; in 1528 he defended the realistic conception in these words: 'It is speaking perfectly appropriately to say, as we display the bread: *"This is the body of Christ."* And whoever looks at the bread sees the Body of Christ, just as John said that he saw the

Holy Spirit, when he saw the dove, as we have heard. The words continue to be appropriate when we say: Whoever takes this bread takes the Body of Christ; and whoever eats this bread eats the Body of Christ; whoever crunches this bread with teeth or tongue crunches the Body of Christ. And it always still remains true that no one sees, takes, eats or crunches the Body of Christ, as other flesh is visibly seen and chewed. For what we do to bread is rightly and reasonably appropriate to the Body of Christ because of the sacramental unity. That is why the visionaries are wrong, as is also the gloss on the canonical law, when they vilify Pope Nicholas because he forced Berengar to confess: 'that he bit and chewed with his teeth the actual Body of Christ.' God grant that all popes have treated all matters in such a Christian spirit as this pope with Berengar in this confession. For the thought is that whoever eats and masticates this bread eats and masticates what is the actual Body of Christ and not merely bread, as Wiclif teaches.' (*Of the Lord's Supper*, Weimar Ed. XXVI.442–443.)

After reading this text no doubt can be cast upon the belief of Luther in the real and living presence of Christ in the Eucharist according to the traditional realist conception, balanced by what he calls 'the sacramental unity.'

5. *The substantialist conception*

In Berengar's oath of 1079, the idea of substance begins to appear to explain and to moderate the realist conception which could be accused of being too carnal a conception: the bread and the wine are 'transformed in substance' to become the body and blood of Christ 'in their own nature and in their actual substance.' It was thanks to Lanfranc, the master of Bec, later Archbishop of Canterbury († 1089) and to Guitmond d'Aversa († 1095) that the substantialist controversy which was to lead to the doctrine of *transubstantiation*, developed. To escape the accusation of an over carnal and physical approach to the Eucharist and to maintain all the realism of Christ's presence, these theologians explained that the substances of the bread and the wine are changed into the profound being of Christ, the essence of his Body and his Blood. 'We believe that the earthy substances are converted into the essence of the body of the Lord.' (Lanfranc, *De Corpore et Sanguine Domini adversus Berengarium,* PL 150.430.) For Guitmond d'Aversa the transformation of substance, which touches the deep, hidden reality, allows the appearances or accidents of the previous reality to subsist: 'The substance of the things is changed, but the taste, the colour and the other sensible accidents which previously existed subsist.' (*De Corporis et Sanguinis Christi veritate in Eucharistia,* PL 149, 1481.)

A century later, this substantialist conception was still taught in the Western Church. Replying to the question of a former archbishop of Lyons on the words of Jesus at the institution of the Lord's Supper, 'When he transubstantiated the bread and the wine into his body and his blood,' Pope Innocent III wrote in 1202: 'In the canon of the mass, we say "*Mystery of the faith*" Because there we believe something other than we see, and see something other than we believe. Indeed, we see the species of bread and wine and we believe the truth of the body and the blood of Christ, and the power of unity and charity . . . Very careful distinction must be made between three things in this sacrament which are different, the visible form, the truth of the body and the spiritual power. The form is the bread and the wine; the truth is the flesh and the blood; the spiritual power is the unity and the charity.' (*Denz. En. Symb.,* 414–415). The eucharistic doctrine finds its almost complete expression in this letter. The Lateran Council, in 1215, confirmed the substantialist conception with its two important objectives: to defend the realism of the presence of Christ and the sacramental mystery of that presence:

'Jesus Christ is himself the priest and the sacrifice, whose body and blood are really present under the species of bread and wine in the sacrament of the altar, the bread being transubstantiated into his body, and the wine into his blood by the divine power, so that we receive from him what he has received from us, to accomplish the mystery of the unity.' (*Denz, En. Symb.,* 430)

St Thomas Aquinas completed this reflection on transubstantiation, by giving it metaphysical arguments which are difficult for a modern mind to grasp. But the content of the doctrine remains the same: the reality of the presence of Christ takes the place of what makes the bread and wine ordinary food and drink:

'Since in this sacrament there is the true body of Christ and it does not begin to be there by a movement of locality; since moreover, as we have shown, the body of Christ is not there as in a place: we are really obliged to affirm that it begins to be there by the conversion of the substance of the bread into it . . . And that is what is produced, by the divine virtue, in this sacrament. For the whole substance of the bread is converted into the whole substance of the body of Christ, and the whole substance of the wine into the whole substance of the blood of Christ. This conversion, therefore, is not of form but of substance. It does not figure among the various kinds of natural movements, but we can call it transubstantiation which is its proper name. (*Summa Theol.* III, Qu.75, Art.4).

6. *The Conception of the Mystery of the Concomitance*

The reformers Luther and Calvin both believe firmly in the real, living presence of Christ in the Lord's Supper. The mode of this presence is of secondary importance for them. When they affirm that the substance of the Eucharist, that is to say its deep fundamental reality, is the body and the blood of Christ, they are not so interested by the manner in which the substance of the bread and the blood of Christ is united and communicated with the signs of the bread and the wine. For them it is important to believe in the total presence of Christ in the Lord's Supper and in the communication of his body and blood; it is not important to know if the substance of the bread and the wine disappear to give place to that of the body and blood of Christ by a transubstantiation. Considering the connection between the substance of bread and wine and the profound reality of the body and blood of Christ present in the Lord's Supper, Luther wrote: 'Although the body and the blood are two different natures, each in itself, and that, when they are separated from one another, the one is certainly not the other, when they are united and become a complete new entity they lose their difference, as far as this new unique being is concerned; and, as they become and are one thing only, we name them and speak of them as one thing only; it is therefore unnecessary for one of them to disappear and be annihilated, but that the two, the bread and the body, should subsist, and because of the sacramental unity we say and rightly: *'This is my body'*, indicating the body with the little word *'this'*. For it is now no longer simply bread from the oven, but bread-body or body-bread, that is to say bread which has become one entity only and one sacramental thing only with the body of Christ. It is the same too with the wine in the cup: *'This is my blood'*, with the little word ' *this"* which indicates the wine. For it is now no longer simply wine from the cellar, but wine-blood, that is to say wine which has become with the blood of Christ one single sacramental entity. Whether the wine is still there or not, enough for me that the blood of Christ is there. Be it with the wine as God wills. And rather than not have anything there but wine, with the "visionaries", I prefer to agree with the pope that there is only blood. Better still I said above that when the wine became Christ's blood, there is not simply wine, but wine-blood, so that I can show it and say "this is the blood of Christ".' (W.XXVI, 445, 462.)

That is a strong affirmation of the mystery of the real presence and the refusal of any philosophical or popular explanation of the link between the substance of the body and the blood of Christ with the signs of bread and wine. This conception has sometimes been called *'consubstantiation.'* The term 'wine-blood' might suggest a name like this. However, the dominant factor in Luther is the affirmation of the mystery and the refusal of any explanation whatsoever. There is rather the conception of a kind of concomitance between the substance of the body and of the blood and the signs of bread and wine.

Calvin has the same conviction that Christ is really present in the Lord's Supper but he too is not interested in the connection between the profound reality or substance and the outward signs. He sees rather in them the means which communicate to us the very substance of the body and blood of Christ:

'If these words are not said for nothing, it is right that, in order to have our life in Christ, our souls should be sated with his body and his blood as with their own food. That is plainly stated to us in the Supper when he says to us of the bread that we should take it and eat it, and that it is his body: that we should drink of the cup and that it is his blood. It is specifically spoken of as the body and the blood, so that we should learn to seek there the substance of our spiritual life.

Now if nevertheless any should ask if the bread is the body of Christ and the wine his blood, we will reply that the bread and the wine are visible signs, which represent to us the body and the blood: but that this name and title of body and blood is attributed to them, so that they are, as it were, instruments by which the Lord Jesus distributes them to us.' (*Petit traité de la sainte cène,* p. 110.) The term 'represent' should be taken here in its strong sense, for Calvin adds a little later: 'the visible signs are not a bare figure, but joined with its truth and substance. So it is right and proper for the bread to be called body, since not only does it represent the body to us, it also presents the body to us.'

These different conceptions of the real and living presence of Christ in the Eucharist are not necessarily contradictory. They may even be complementary. We have seen how in the early Church the metabolist and the sacramentalist conceptions balanced one another. When the realism became aggravated and ran the risk of becoming a fleshly conception, the idea of substance arose to indicate a change in the profound reality allowing the outward signs to subsist. Would it not even be possible to admit, in the unity of the eucharistic belief, both ideas, transubstantiation and concomitance, as possible approaches to the same mystery which remains always unfathomable. But it is evident that these different conceptions can only be complementary when they imply a fundamental common belief whose elements must be analysed.

The Council of Trent (13th Session, 1551) endeavoured to define for the Catholic Church the elements necessary for eucharistic belief. Given the polemical climate of the Reformation, some aspects became hardened: today they can be held in balance after the theological labours around the Second Vatican Council. The elements of the basic belief in the Eucharist, defined by the Council of Trent, may be resumed as follows:

(1) The Eucharist is a *sacrament,* the visible sign of an invisible reality, the unfathomable and worshipful mystery of the presence of Christ in his entirety, true God and true man.
(2) After the consecration of the bread and the wine, Christ is *present, truly, really and substantially,* under the figure of these tangible elements.
(3) By the consecration the *conversion* of the profound reality (substance) of the bread and the wine into the profound reality (substance) of the body and the blood of Christ is effected: this conversion is rightly and properly called 'transubstantiation' by the Catholic Church.
(4) The bread and the wine remain the body and blood of Christ after the celebration of the Eucharist and may be taken to the sick: the Eucharist may be *kept* in churches for this purpose.
(5) The sacrament of the Eucharist, instituted to be food, may also be the object of a cult of *worship,* since faith recognizes in it the very presence of Christ as God.

These are the essential points of the Catholic faith affirmed at the Council of Trent. Beyond polemics and in the present ecumenical atmosphere, these points may be used as terms of reference at a conference of Christians, in so far as they are positive in their affirmation of the faith, and provided we disregard the aggressive tone of the council's anathemas.

The two first points on the sacrament and the presence have remained common to all Christians, even through the crisis of the Reformation and of the Counter Reformation. We will see later what meaning should be attached to the adverbs which specify the presence of Christ: 'truly', 'really' and 'substantially'. We have already noted that for Calvin also, the notion of substance allied to the signs was part of the eucharistic doctrine.

The third point on the conversion has become problematic by reason of the scholastic explanations about the substance (profound reality) and the accidents (appearances of the signs), which have complicated the doctrine of transubstantiation which formally made its appearance towards the end of the eleventh century (Lanfranc and Guitmond d'Aversa: 'substantial transformation'), and defined at the 4th Lateran Council, in 1215: 'The bread and the wine are transubstantiated into the body and into the blood of Christ by the divine power.' For Luther, the scholastic explanation of transubstantiation seems too rational for faith in the adorable mystery of the real and living presence of Christ. Calvin too was to resist the scholastic subtleties surrounding the doctrine of transubstantiation, without however refusing the idea of conversion:

'*This is my body.* I do not reject what some say, that by these words the bread was consecrated to be made a sign of the flesh of Christ, provided we give this word "*consecrated*" its full and proper meaning. And so, the bread which was intended to nourish our bodies, is taken by Christ and sanctified to another use, so that it begins to be spiritual food. And that is the conversion or change spoken of by the early Doctors of the Church . . .' (there follows a criticism of scholastic teaching on transubstantiation: *Comm. sur le N.T, vol. 1, 1555*). A revaluation of the doctrine of transubstantiation in an ecumenical sense is a possibility today (cf. F. J. Leenhardt, *Ceci est mon corps*).

On the fourth and fifth points, ecumenical texts of doctrinal convergences (*Faith and Order, Groupe des Dombes*) have attempted to reconcile conceptions which had long been antagonistic concerning the reservation of the consecrated bread and the veneration of the Eucharist outside of the celebration. From what text of Scripture and by what dogmatic right could it be affirmed that the real and living presence of Christ ceases to be one with the sacramental signs, as soon as the celebration of the Eucharist has ended? Does not the promise of Christ also envisage the communion of the sick and the absent, who are also part of the eucharistic community? The answer to these questions could well be a test of authentic belief in the real and living presence of Christ in the Eucharist. Can there be eucharistic faith agreeing with Scripture and the ancient Tradition of the Church if there is no respect for the signs of the Body and the Blood of Christ after the Eucharist has been celebrated?

Practices of venerating and adoring the Eucharist, outside of the celebration, appeared fairly late and slowly in the Western Church. The reaction to the crisis brought about by Berengar de Tours, and the great affirmations of the realist theologians were to favour the beginnings of genuine adoration of the holy sacrament at the Abbey of Bec and at Cluny, as well as in the monasteries under their influence, some external practices of veneration of the Eucharist were initiated about the middle of the eleventh century: kneeling and censing before the reserved species. And during the next three centuries genuine eucharistic devotion developed, culminating, but not until the middle of the fourteenth century, in a considerable increase of prayer before the reserved sacrament. Should we not see in this slow development an indication that we should leave some freedom as far as eucharistic devotion outside of the celebration is concerned, whatever the spiritual fruits received by those who practise it faithfully and fervently?

As regards respect for the eucharistic signs which display faith in the Real Presence, a beautiful passage from Origen testifies to the living devotion of the early Church:

'I would like to exhort you by means of examples drawn from your religious practices. You are in the habit of participating in the various mysteries, and you know with what respect and care you keep the Body of the Lord when it is given to you, for fear a few crumbs should fall and some of the consecrated treasure be lost. For you would count yourselves guilty and rightly so, if by your carelessness, any particle was lost. If then, your approach to his Body is so scrupulous, and rightly so, why should you consider that an attitude of indifference to the Word of God should deserve a lesser punishment than an attitude to his Body?' (*Hom. in Ex.* XIII.3.)

AN ECUMENICAL APPROACH TO THE MYSTERY

As the Church has continued throughout the centuries to reflect afresh on the eucharistic mystery by which she lives at the very heart of her life, she has found her reflection brought to silence, transformed into adoration, so true it is that the Eucharist will always remain a mystery, unfathomable, ineffable and adorable. Pope John Paul II has well expressed how impossible it is to understand and explain this mystery:

'We can say with certainty that the teaching (of the Church), developed with penetration by the theologians, by men of deep faith and prayer, and by ascetics and mystics in their total fidelity to the eucharistic mystery, in reality goes no further than the threshold, because it is incapable of grasping and translating into words what the Eucharist is in its fullness, what it expresses and what is realized in it. In the proper sense of the word it is the ineffable sacrament!' (Enc. *Redemptor Hominis*, 20).

Every attempt to understand by faith this great mystery of the real and living presence of Christ, can only be an approach, instinct with the spirit of adoration. It is by the celebration and the communion rather than by reflection that we can begin to understand all that God gives to the Church through the Eucharist.

1. *The eucharistic presence*

God is present in various ways to his Church and to the believer: he is present in the intimacy of private prayer; he is present in the gathering together of Christians in his Name, he is present when his Word is proclaimed; he is present at the celebration of the Sacraments; he is present in the Eucharist . . .

'When you pray', said Christ, 'withdraw into your room, shut the door, and pray to your Father who is there, in secret, and your Father who sees in secret, shall reward you'. (Matth. 6.6.) It is humble seeking in private, intimate contemplation that has the promise of the presence of God who chooses the way of humility rather than of demonstrations which are too external. This presence is manifested through secret, silent intimacy with the Father, who rewards the humble believer by hearing his prayer and giving him inner peace and perfect joy (John 2.29).

'When two or three are met in my Name, I am there among them', said Christ (Matth. 18.20). The meeting together of the smallest number of believers, members of the Body of Christ, is assured of the presence of the Risen Christ. This presence is manifested in the unity and the charity which makes these differing people one body as they meet to pray together or to act communally.

"Whoever listens to you listens to me,' said Jesus to the seventy-two disciples. 'Whoever rejects you, rejects me and whoever rejects me rejects the One who sent me.' (Luke 10.16.) The faithful proclamation of the Word of God carries within itself the presence of God who speaks to his people and to each of the faithful. God himself makes use of the language of words as a means to convey his presence to the mind and the heart, awakening and developing faith with them.

On the evening of Easter Day, the Risen Christ breathed on the disciples and said: 'Receive the Holy Spirit; those whose sins you forgive will be forgiven; the sins you retain, will be retained.' (John 20, 22–23.) The sacraments or the sacramental actions of the Church are visible and effective signs which manifest concretely the presence of Christ and his power to regenerate and sanctify by the Holy Spirit. God uses material elements; water, bread, wine, oil, the laying-on the hands . . . displayed in significant actions as channels of his effective presence and transforms the whole being of the believer.

The Eucharist carries the presence of Christ in a unique way which cannot be compared with any other mode of the presence of God. Jesus spoke words over the bread and the wine of the Eucharist: *This is my body . . . this is my blood . . .*' What Christ said is the truth and it is accomplished every time the Eucharist is celebrated. The Church confesses the real, living and acting presence of Christ in the Eucharist. By the very words of Jesus and by the power of the Holy Spirit, the bread and the wine of the Eucharist become the sacrament of the body and blood of the Risen Christ, that is of the living Christ present in all his fullness. The profound reality under the signs of bread and wine, is the whole being of Christ who comes to us to feed us and to transform our whole being.

The presence of Christ in the Eucharist is a personal presence which enters into a personal relationship with those who believe and receive. The eucharistic presence is neither a thing nor an object, it is a relationship of person to person. A piece of furniture is not *present* in a room it is *simply there*. People can be very near to one another, even crowded together in one place, in a bus, for instance, without being present to one another, they too, like objects, can be simply there, relative to one another. If, for example, an accident happens and someone is hurt, others are concerned about him, they look after him and help him, then these people who were simply there become present to one another because as persons they enter into relationship with one another: the being present of each one of them coincides with the presence of the other: from being objects in juxtaposition they become present to one another in a truly personal relationship.

However, this personal relationship between people, this being present of each one of them, the coinciding of their being present, cannot occur without the mediation of our bodies by which we give each other personal signs of being present.

The presence of Christ in the Eucharist is the personal presence of the Risen Christ, who enters into relationship with the personal reality of each Christian, makes his being present coincide with the being present of each one. The means of mediation of this personal relationship of Christ with those who receive him is his resurrection body, present and manifest under the signs of bread and wine: the resurrection body becomes the eucharistic body in order to establish personal relationship between Christ and the faithful, through their bodies, of which he becomes the supernatural food.

2. *The presence of the body and the blood of Christ*

The presence of Christ in the Eucharist is the presence of his body and of his blood: '*This is my body . . . This is the cup of my* blood . . .' Why this double mention of the body and the blood? The naming of the body and the blood separately is a sign of Christ's sacrifice. In the blood sacrifice of the Old Testament, the separation of the body and the blood of the victim was an important evocative sign. And so, when, at the first Lord's Supper, Christ spoke of his body and of his blood, the disciples saw before their eyes, under the signs of the bread and of the wine, the evocation of a sacrifice. As they celebrated the Passover meal, it was quite naturally the sacrifice. As they celebrated the Passover meal, it was quite naturally the sacrifice of the Lamb which came to their minds: Jesus became for them the Passover Lamb, about to be sacrificed to inaugurate the New Covenant. The Church would recognize in the Eucharist the memorial, the sacrament or the presence of the sacrifice of Christ offered up on the cross as the new Passover Lamb, because he came to her under the signs of the bread and wine, signs of the body and the blood of the victim offered up for the salvation of the world and the inauguration of the New Covenant. And so, in the very existence of the two elements of bread and of wine, signs of the body and the blood, we have the sacrament of the sacrifice on the cross, as we have the sacrament of the body and of the blood of Christ separately, the sacrament of a victim sacrificed. By the Eucharist, the Church makes actual the unique sacrifice of the cross and all its sanctifying power, under the separate signs of the bread and the wine, which are the body and the blood of Christ, separated at his death.

If the Eucharist were nothing but the sacrament of the real and living presence of the Risen Christ, one element would be sufficient to communicate it to us; Christ is not divided and the fullness of his being is communicated to us in one species alone. But the Eucharist is also the sacrament of Christ's sacrifice; it is the real and living presence of Christ who was crucified for us. Then *the celebration and communion in two species* can be understood. The Church accomplishes the memorial of the sacrifice on the cross, signified by the separation of the body and the blood of Christ, and she enters into communion with this sacrifice by taking the bread and the wine, the body and the blood of Christ, separately. The communion in two species is therefore a communion of Christ who is really present as the one who offered himself in sacrifice, with all the power which flows from this sacrifice, the communion under separate signs of his body and of his blood, as the Passover Lamb sacrificed.

But it is, obviously, as the Crucified Risen One that Christ is present. The risen body of Christ transcended the normal limitations of human bodies: as proofs we have the appearances of the Risen Lord to his disciples in a room with the doors shut, to Mary Magdalene who took him for a gardener, to the two disciples at Emmaus who did not recognize him until he broke the bread . . . St Paul distinguishes between the physical body, which obeys the natural laws of this world, and the spiritual body, imbued with the *pneuma,* the divine breath, the Holy Spirit, who is incorruptible, immortal and glorious, liberated from the laws of terrestrial matter (1 Cor. 15.44–49).

The body of the Risen Christ remains a body in the sense that it can make itself visible, as to the disciples at Easter, that it can make contact with other bodies, the bodies of the believers and the sharers in communion, that it can make its being-present coincide with their being-present, in the Eucharist, to touch them and to be given to them. The body of the Risen Christ, the concrete presence of the total Christ makes use of the signs of the bread and the wine, consecrated in the Eucharist to manifest itself and to act in the Church. When Christ repeats in the Eucharist: 'This is my body . . .', that means: this consecrated bread serves me as a body, me the Risen One, so that I may be bodily present among you, as I was among the disciples after Easter, so that I may be perceived in a tangible way and received concretely. In the Eucharist the body of the Risen Christ is identified with the consecrated bread and wine, it becomes a eucharistic body in order to communicate to us the fullness of its life.

The body of the Risen Christ which becomes a eucharistic body, transmits to the believer who receives it the very life of God, the energy of his being and the light of his glory. The body and the blood of Christ are not things offered for our passive contemplation. They are eternal life communicated to people.

'I am the living bread, come down from heaven,' said Christ; 'anyone who eats this bread shall live for ever; and the bread that I shall give him is my flesh for the life of the world . . . Whoever eats my flesh and drinks my blood has eternal life and I will resurrect him on the last day . . . Whoever eats my flesh and drinks my blood dwells in me and I in him'. (John 6.51. 54. 56.)

3. Truly, really, substantially

These three adverbs, retained by the Council of Trent to qualify the mode of the presence of Christ in the Eucharist, we can find textually or otherwise expressed in Luther and Calvin. They represent an attempt to approach the mystery of the faith, that eucharistic mystery which will always remain ineffable and adorable.

The first adverb refers to the *truth* of the gift of God in the Eucharist: when Christ says that here he gives us his body, it is because in truth his Risen Body is present and is given. Truth is there in opposition to the image, the simple figure the purely external sign which would send us back to a distant reality, absent from us now.

Calvin explained it in this way:

'Jesus Christ attests to us and seals in the sacrament that participation in his flesh and his blood, by which he pours his life into us, just as if he were entering into the very marrow of our bones. He does not present us with an empty frustrating sign, but displays in it the power of his Spirit to accomplish what he promises . . . This is why the Apostle says that the bread we break is the communion of the body of Christ, and the cup we consecrate by the words of the Gospel and the prayers, is the communion of his blood (1 Cor. 10.16). No one should object that this is a figure of speech in which the name of the thing represented is attributed to the sign . . .'

Calvin then pursues his argument by emphasizing strongly the polarity of 'the truth' of the sign and what he considers simply a figure:

'We can deduce from the fact that the sign is given to us, that *the substance* is also conveyed *in its truth*. For if somebody has no intention of calling God a deceiver, they will not dare to say that it is a vain and empty sign of *his truth* which he in truth is offering. That is why if the Lord is for us the participation of his body in the breaking of the bread there can be no doubt that he is giving us at the same time that participation. And in fact, the faithful should make a hard and fast rule, that every time they see the signs God has ordained, they can know for certain that *the truth* of the thing represented is incorporated, and be convinced of that . . . we should be confident beyond all shadow of doubt *that when we take the sign of the body we are taking the body itself.* (*Inst. Chret.* IV, XVII, 10.)

Luther makes a still more vigorous stand against the visionaries or sacramentarians, disciples of Wiclif and Zwingli, on the truth of the presence of the risen body of Christ beneath the external signs of the Eucharist (*Of the Lord's Supper*, W. XXVI, 395–399).

And so, for the Reformers as for the Council of Trent, the truth of the sacrament of the Eucharist, founded on the Word of God, excludes any possibility of being purely a symbol of a distant reality or merely the energy from an action in the past. In the eucharistic signs, there is the truth of the presence of the risen body of Christ.

The second adverb refers to the *reality* of God's gift in the Eucharist: if the body of the Risen Christ is really present in the Eucharist, it is present objectively, independently of the subjectivity and even of the faith of the celebrants, the believers and those who receive. The reality is in contrast here with the imagination, the subjectivity, the faith of individuals and the moral worthiness which might be thought to deserve God's gift. The body of the Risen Christ is present under the eucharistic signs by reason of the promise of Jesus at the institution of the Last Supper: '*This is my body . . . This is the cup of my blood . . . Do this as a memorial of me.*' It is present by the power of the Holy Spirit who responds to the invocation or epiclesis of the Church and who sanctifies the eucharistic elements and makes them the signs of the body and the blood of Christ, the sacrament or the presence of his risen body. The Word and the Spirit assure the objective reality of the presence of Christ. Certainly faith is necessary for this presence to bear all its fruits of sanctification in the receiver and in the Church, but it is not the faith that brings the presence of Christ: that would be to attribute a value of merit to faith, which is contrary to the Gospel; faith merits nothing, it receives the grace of God and bears its fruits. Faith does not make Christ present: faith receives him in the Eucharist and allows this communion to bear fruit. It is the Word of God and the Holy Spirit that bring the real and objective presence of the risen body of Christ under the signs of the bread and the wine they sanctify. By the words of the Lord at the Last Supper and by the epiclesis of the Holy Spirit upon the Church and the Eucharist, the bread and the wine become the figure, the sign and the sacrament of the risen body of Jesus Christ really and objectively present. 'It is absolutely not by imagination or by thought that we receive it, but its substance is truly given.' (Calvin, *ibid*, 19.)

The third adverb refers to *the substance* of the Risen Lord's body under the signs of the consecrated bread and wine: the body of the Risen Lord is *truly* present, not only figuratively, it is *really* present, objectively and not only in the subjectivity of faith, it is present *substantially*, that is to say according to a particular mode, unique to the eucharistic mystery. The consecrated bread and wine are no longer ordinary food and drink, they have become the outward signs of a profound new reality which is the risen body of Christ, truly and really present. The substance means here, in the etymological sense of the word 'what stands underneath', it is the profound reality of its being which causes it to be what it is and not something else. Being can change its substance, or its profound reality, and becoming something else. Let us take first an example from everyday life. Wool becomes, by means of the human work of spinning and weaving, a fabric which in its turn by means of the work of cutting and sewing, can become a garment. The fabric, the wool, is present at every stage, there is no chemical change that takes place between the sheep's wool and the cloth, the cloth and the garment. But the profound reality, the substance, and the end product have changed from one, into the other. A fleece has become a piece of cloth and the cloth has become a garment. Even if the matter and its properties, the wool and the heat it can promote, have not changed, the end product and the substance, or the profound reality, have been transformed irreversibly; the garment made to clothe a man cannot turn back into cloth to be sold, nor can it turn into a fleece for the sheep. The substance has been modified, the chemical matter and its properties have remained: the fleece has become cloth, then garment, while the wool and its heat have been maintained.

The liturgical words of the offertory, in the Eucharist, can make us understand the meaning of the substantial presence of the body of Christ under the signs of the bread and of the wine. *'Blessed are you, Lord, God of all creation. Through your goodness we have this bread to offer, which earth has given and human hands have made. It will become for us the bread of life.'* The

57

wheat, fruit of earth, becomes bread, by the labour of men: by the work of the Word of God and the Holy Spirit this bread will become the body of the Risen Lord, the Bread of Life eternal. At each stage the flour as matter with nourishing properties for mankind is still present. But the substance has changed from one into the other: by man's labour seeds of grain have become bread, bread to be used as ordinary food; this bread by the work of the Word and the Spirit will become the body of the Risen Christ, food of eternal life. The substance, or the profound reality of the seed of the wheat may possibly become flour or seed corn for more wheat. The substance of bread is to be the ordinary food of many people. The substance of eucharistic bread is to be the risen body of Christ given as food that sanctifies and transmits eternal life. The transformation of the substance of the wheat into bread is irreversible, by reason of the various labours of men; the bread can never become grain again although it has retained its matter and properties. The conversion of the bread into the sacrament or presence of the body of Christ, who has become the substance of profound reality of this consecrated bread is just as irreversible because of the work of the Word of God and the Holy Spirit. God never goes back on what he has given.

4. *Approximate images*

The real and living presence of the risen body of Christ remains a mystery we can only approach from afar off. However, the theologians have put forward some comparisons which can help our thinking in its approach, but these images are always approximations and cannot exhaust the understanding of the mystery.

The Reformers ran into difficulties caused by the ideas of their times, and they offered some images to suggest an answer to their questions. Calvin saw that one problem lay in 'the nature of a human body' which the risen Christ possesses, in the fact that he is in heaven and that he cannot therefore be 'degraded among the corruptible elements.' He imagines therefore that our actual participation in the body of Christ is effected by the Holy Spirit who is compared to the sun's rays which communicate warmth and life:

'The place of this conjoining (with the body of Christ) is

therefore the Holy Spirit, by whom we are joined together: he is like the channel or the duct by which all that Christ is or has descends to us. For if our eyes perceive that the sun shining upon the earth sends down by its rays something of its substance to engender and nourish the fruits of this earth and to make them grow, why should the light and the radiance of the Spirit of Jesus Christ be any less able to communicate to us his flesh and his blood' (*Inst. Chrét*, IV, XVII 12.)

This comparison, interesting as it is, arises from a conception of the universe which bears the stamp of the science of its day and does not make sufficient allowance for the change effected by the resurrection on the body of Christ. The interesting thing about this image is the part given to the Holy Spirit in the actualization of the mystery of the presence of Christ through the eucharistic signs.

Luther put forward several comparisons to convince his opponents who denied the real presence of Christ in the Eucharist, since his human body has to be in one definite place.

'If a mirror had been broken into a thousand pieces, the entire image which appeared before in the entire mirror would still remain in each of the pieces . . . The sun shines upon a lake or a pond. Of course, there can only be one image of the sun on the water, for there is only one sun. How does it come about then, that if a hundred and yet another hundred people were standing round the lake, each one of them would have before him the image of the sun at the place where he is and not at the other man's place? . . . When there is a column in the square, even although thousands and thousands of eyes are around looking at it, every eye perceives the whole column in its vision . . . One single voice is at the same time instantaneously in the mouth of the preacher and in all the ears of the people, as if his mouth and their ears were one place where the voice was without any intermediary . . .' (*Of the Lord's Supper*, W. XXVI, 337–338, 415–416.)

All these traditionally well known comparisons come up against the mystery of the resurrected body of Christ which no one is able to imagine.

The last of Luther's images, the voice of the preacher carried on sound waves, is certainly the most modern and it approaches the mystery the most closely. The images carried nowadays together with words on waves, allow a man to be seen and heard across the whole world, to be present simultaneously in the homes of millions of people and to communicate to them by his face and his speech the message he intends for them.

The Risen Christ, his body and his entire being can be really and substantially present in all the Eucharists of the Church, under the figure, sign or sacrament of the bread and the wine, consecrated by the Word of God which is a true promise, and by the Holy Spirit who is a real power. Those who hold the substantial presence of the resurrected body of Christ in the Eucharist to be the profound reality of the consecrated species, meet various difficulties according as to how they envisage the relationship between the body of Christ and the eucharistic signs.

For the scholastics and the Council of Trent, who affirm transubstantiation, the difficulty, or the mystery, lies in the conception of bread which has nothing but the outward appearance of bread and whose substance has given place or been changed into the substance of the body of Christ. How can the species or the outward appearance of bread remain without leaving the substance of the bread but only the substance of the body of Christ? In scholastic language, how can the accidents of the bread remain without the substance of the bread?

In the Encyclical *Mysterium Fidei*, Paul VI, in 1965, expressed this doctrine afresh:

'Once the nature or substance of the bread and the wine have been changed into the body and the blood of Christ, nothing subsists of the bread and the wine but the species only, under which Christ in this entirety is present in this physical, and even bodily reality, although in a mode of presence different from that by which bodies occupy this or that place.'

Faced with the difficulties of the scholastic explantion of transubstantiation, the Franciscan theologian Duns Scotus (†1308) posed the question of liberty of interpretation of the eucharistic mystery: 'Since the true Principle of each and every thing is the divine Power alone, in what way is consubstantiation, which permits the substance of the bread and that of the body to coexist, a less valid possibility than transubstantiation which effects the conversion of the first into the second or even annihilation which suppresses the substance of the bread? Miracle for miracle, which is preferable?' (G. Martelet, *Résurrection, eucharistie et genèse de l'homme*, 1972, p. 154.)

Luther was not far from posing the same questions; for him the difficulty, or the mystery, was in understanding how the bread can remain with the body of Christ, how there can possibly be concomitance of the substance of the resurrected body of Christ and the substance of the bread and the wine; 'I hold against all reason and all high logic that two distinct beings can be and can be called one single being' (*Of the Lord's Supper* XXVI. 439.) He seeks justifications in the mystery of the Trinity: 'If the unity of the nature and of the being can, in this instance, cause distinct persons to be spoken of nevertheless as one and the same being, it can certainly not be contrary to Scripture and to the articles of the faith that two distinct objects, such as the bread and the body are said to be one or one sole being.' (ibid. 440). Luther also instances the mystery of the two natures, the human and the divine, which are one in the person of Christ. If we name the humanity of Christ declaring: This is the Son of God; it is not necessary for his humanity to disappear or to be changed into divinity; on the contrary, the christological faith of the Church affirms the permanence of the humanity and the divinity in the unity of the person of Christ, who is at the same time God and man. Why could the same mystery not take place with the concomitance of the substance of the bread and that of the resurrected body of Christ?

We have seen that for Calvin the difficulty, or the mystery, was to comprehend how the body of the Risen Christ glorified in heaven can be with the bread in the Eucharist, and it is here that he appeals to the action of the Holy Spirit, 'by which all that Christ is and has descends to us.'

The weakness of all the images, the explanations and difficulties, arises from the fact that the mystery of the resurrected body of Christ always eludes our comprehension. On the other hand, we cannot place the substance of the bread and that of Christ's body on the same plane. It is not a question of one object taking the place of another object; it is the very person of the Risen Lord who by means of his resurrected body, which becomes eucharistic, makes himself present to the Church under the outward signs of bread and wine. The substance of bread and wine is to be food and drink for people, it is to carry a specific meaning and to exist for a specific earthly purpose; the substance of the risen body of Christ, is to be the very life of God: 'Anyone who eats my flesh and drinks my blood has eternal life and I will raise him up at the last day.' (John 6.54.) These two profound realities are not comparable, they are dissymmetrical: the conversion of one into the other is therefore an assumption in which what was terrestrial is absorbed into the life of the resurrected body of Christ. Perhaps it is the language of 'clothing' which is most suitable to express the mystery of the conversion of the eucharistic signs into the Body of Christ in the sense in which St Paul applies it to the resurrection: 'I am going to tell you a mystery: we shall not all die, but we all shall be transformed . . . Indeed this corruptible being must clothe itself in incorruptibility, and this mortal being clothe itself in immortality.' (1 Cor. 15.51–53.)

In the Eucharist, the bread and the wine, terrestrial and corruptible nutrients, destined to be physical food for men, must be transformed and clothe the Body of the Risen Christ, be taken up and absorbed in him to become signs and powers of resurrection, incorruptibility and immortality.

5. *Basic points for an ecumenical doctrine*

Over the bread and the wine of the Eucharist, Jesus said: *'This is my body .,. . This is my blood . . .'* The Church has always understood these words in a realistic sense: what Christ said is the truth and is accomplished every time the Eucharist is celebrated. By the very words of Jesus and by the power of the Holy Spirit, the bread and the wine of the Eucharist become the body and the blood of the Risen Christ, that is to say, the living Christ, in his entire person.

By a mysterious conversion, the bread and the wine become Christ himself, who unites himself in substance with these visible signs: and so the presence of Christ in the Eucharist is unique, irreducible to any other form of presence. Under the outward signs of the bread and the wine, the profound reality is the total being of Christ, entering into bodily contact with man to nourish him and to transform him in his whole being.

The Church confesses the real, living and acting presence of Christ in the Eucharist. The discernment of the body and the blood of Christ requires faith. And yet, the real presence of

Christ in the Eucharist does not depend on each person's faith, for it is Christ who unites himself, by his Word and the power of the Holy Spirit, to the eucharistic elements, the signs that his presence has been given.

The bread and the wine consecrated in the Eucharist are no longer ordinary food and drink: their meaning, their finality, their substance and their profound reality have been transformed to become the body and the blood of Christ. The resurrected body of Christ assumes and absorbs the eucharistic elements so that they become the signs and the power of his real and living presence; philosophical reflection on the idea of substance is secondary. It is enough to affirm that the profound reality of the bread and of the wine is no longer to be earthly food and drink, but the resurrection body of Christ which takes a eucharistic figure. Under the outward signs of the eucharistic species, the body of the Risen Christ is present truly, really and substantially.

This presence is true, it is not a purely symbolic figure, this presence is real, it is not merely subjective imagination; this presence is substantial: it is tied up with the profound reality of the signs of the bread and of the wine.

The presence of the resurrection body of Christ remains united with the eucharistic signs, for the Church does not dispose of this presence which is the fruit of the Word of God and of the action of the Holy Spirit. By what right would she determine the time when the species of the bread and of the wine would no longer be the signs of the body and the blood of Christ? That would be contrary to belief in the efficacious grace of God. 'The gifts and the calling of God are irreversible.' (Rom. 11.29.) The certainty that the presence of Christ continues after the celebration and the communion, under the species of the remaining bread and wine is an important sign of belief in the Eucharist. It is by the Word of God and the action of the Holy Spirit that the bread and the wine have become the sacrament of the body and the blood of Christ. 'They are from then onwards, in their ultimate truth under the outward sign, the reality which has been given, and that they remain with a view to their consumption. What is given as the body and blood of Christ remains given as the body and blood of Christ and demands to be treated as such'. (*Groupe des Dombes*).

The invocation
of the Spirit
upon the Eucharist

The liturgy of the Eucharist comprises an invocation of the Holy Spirit, or epiclesis, upon the celebration, the bread and the wine, and the ecclesiastical assembly, which manifests the dependence of the Church in relation to God, in every sacrament, as in her whole life.

Traditionally the *epiclesis* is found either *before* Christ's words of the institution (This is my body . . . This is the cup of my blood . . .), manifesting the action of the Spirit which makes actual and efficacious the word of the Son to the glory of the Father, or *after* the anamnesis of the mysteries of salvation, manifesting the gift of the Spirit who completes the work of the Father and of the Son, or in a few cases both *before* the institution *and after* the anamnesis, manifesting the role of the Spirit who constitutes the sacramental body of Christ *and* the ecclesial body. Concerning the texts produced below, the reader will notice, between brackets, the position of the epiclesis in the eucharistic prayer, before the institution or after the anamnesis.

EARLY LITURGIES

Hippolytus, *Apostolic Tradition* (c. 215) (after the anamnesis)

We ask you to send your Holy Spirit into the offering of Holy Church; grant, as you gather them together, to all the saints receiving, to be filled with the Holy Spirit so as to affirm their

67

faith in truth, that we may praise and glorify you through your Child Jesus *Christ, through whom glory and honour be paid to you Father, and to the Son, with the Holy Spirit in Holy Church, now and for evermore. Amen.*

The Apostolic Constitutions (c. 380)

We pray you to regard with favour these offerings we have laid before you, God, who have no need of anything; may they be pleasing in your sight to the honour of your Christ; we pray you also to send upon this sacrifice your Holy Spirit, who witnessed the sufferings of the Lord Jesus, that he may reveal that this bread is the body of your Christ and this cup the blood of your Christ; that all who share in them may be strengthened in devotion, find remission of sins, be protected from the devil and the error of his ways, be filled with the Holy Spirit, become worthy of your Christ and obtain eternal life with your reconciliation, O Lord almighty.

LITURGIES OF THE ALEXANDRIAN TYPE

Euchologion of Serapion

(between the Sanctus and the institution:)
Heaven and earth are full of your great glory, Lord of all power: fill this sacrifice also with your power and your communion; for it is to you that we have offered this living sacrifice, this sacrifice without blood . . .

(After the institution:)
God of truth, let your holy Logos come upon this bread, that the bread may become the body of the Logos, and on this cup, that the cup may become the blood of the Truth . . .

Fragment of Dêr – Balyzeh (sixth century)
(witness of the liturgy of Saint Mark)

(between the Sanctus and the institution:)

Fill us also with the glory that comes from you, and deign to send your Holy Spirit upon these creatures: make this bread the body of

our Lord and Saviour Jesus Christ, And as this bread scattered . . .
(the text of the modified Didache follows)

(institution, then gap; then: second epiclesis:)
. . . grant to us your servants the power of the Holy Spirit, the
strengthening and increase of faith, the hope of eternal life.

LITURGIES OF THE ANTIOCHENE TYPE

Anaphora of St Basil (fourth century)
(after the anamnesis)

*Most holy Master, we sinners and your unworthy servants, have
been considered worthy to serve at your holy altar, not because of
our goodness for we have done nothing good on earth – but because
of your compassion and your mercies, which you shed abundantly
upon us; in confidence we approach your holy altar, and having
laid before you the 'antitypes' of the sacred body of the blood of your
Christ, we pray you and we invoke you, Holiest of the holy, by your
goodness and your kindness, let your most holy Spirit come upon us
and upon these gifts before you, that he may bless them and sanctify
them, that he may consecrate this bread: the precious body of our
Lord, God and Saviour Jesus Christ, Amen, and this cup: the
precious blood of our Lord, God and Saviour Jesus Christ, Amen,
shed for the life of the whole world, Amen.*

*May all we who share in the one bread and the cup be united to
one another in the communion of the one Holy Spirit, and that none
of us may share in the sacred body and in the blood of your Christ to
his own judgement or condemnation, but that we may find compassion and grace with all the saints who were pleasing to you since the
beginning, the early fathers, the patriarchs, prophets, apostles,
preachers, evangelists, martyrs, confessors, doctors, all the righteous
in the Spirit, who remained in the faith to the end.*

Anaphora of St John Chrysostom (fourth century.)
(after the anamnesis:)

*We offer you this spiritual worship without blood sacrifice and
we invoke you, we pray to you and we beseech you: send your Holy
Spirit upon us and on these gifts before you, and make this bread
the precious body of your Christ, changing it by your Holy Spirit,*

69

Amen, that they may become for those who participate, purification of the soul, remission of sins, communion of the Holy Spirit, fullness of the Kingdom, confidence before you, and not judgement or condemnation.

LITURGY OF THE SYRO-ORIENTAL TYPE

Anaphora of the Apostles (Addai and Mari)
(at the end of the eucharistic prayer:)

May your Holy Spirit come, Lord, and may he rest upon the oblation of your servants, may he bless it and sanctify it: may it give us, Lord, the forgiveness of sins, the great hope of the resurrection of the dead and new life in the kingdom of heaven with all those who were pleasing to you.

WESTERN LITURGIES

Roman canon
(equivalents of the prayer of epiclesis.)
(a) At the offertory (*Veni, sanctificator . . .*)
Come, Sanctifier, eternal and almighty God, and bless this sacrifice prepared for your holy name.
(b) Before the institution (*Quam oblationem . . .*)
Bless and approve our offering; make it acceptable to you, an offering in spirit and in truth. Let it become for us the body and blood of Jesus Christ, your only Son, our Lord.
(c) After the anamnesis (*Supplices te . . .*)
Almighty God, we pray that your angel may take this sacrifice to your altar in heaven. Then as we receive from this altar the sacred body and blood of your Son, let us be filled with every grace and blessing.

Gallican liturgy
(*collectio post secreta,* after the institution, *Missa de Adventu:*)

God almighty, we beseech you, let your holy Word descend upon these offerings, may the Spirit of your great glory descend, may the gift of your continual mercy descend, that this sacrifice may become spiritual worship, pleasing to you: and may your victorious hand protect us your servants by the blood of Christ.

70

EUCHARISTIC PRAYERS OF THE PRESENT DAY

A. *Roman Catholic*
(before the institution and after the anamnesis as in the liturgies of the Alexandrian type)

Second Eucharistic Prayer (inspired by Hippolytus)

Let your Spirit come upon these gifts to make them holy, so that they may become for us the body and blood of our Lord, Jesus Christ . . . May all of us who share in the body and blood of Christ be brought together in unity by the Holy Spirit.

Third Eucharistic Prayer

And so Father, we bring you these gifts. We ask you to make them holy by the power of your Spirit, that they may become the body and blood of your Son, our Lord Jesus Christ, at whose command we celebrate this eucharist.

Fourth Eucharistic Prayer

Father, may the Holy Spirit sanctify these offerings. Let them become the body and blood of Jesus Christ our Lord. . .
Lord, look upon this sacrifice which you have given to your Church: and by your Holy Spirit, gather all who share this bread and wine into the one body of Christ . . .

Swiss Catholic Synod

And so we pray you, Father almighty, send your Spirit upon this bread and this wine, that Christ Jesus may realize in our midst the presence of his Body and of his Blood . . . God, loving Father, give us the Spirit of love, the Spirit of your Son.

B. *Ambrosian Catholics* (Milan)
(before the institution: epiclesis of the Spirit; after: epiclesis of the Son).

Fifth Eucharistic Prayer

And we, being raised to the dignity of being able to present to you, by the efficacy of the Holy Spirit, the sublime sacrifice of the body and of the blood of our Lord . . . Send us, O Almighty Father, your only Son . . .

Sixth Eucharistic Prayer

With a love that knows no limits he (Christ) has left us this sacrifice to offer to your name: his body and his blood, which the power of the Holy Spirit makes present on the altar . . . Send among us, in this sacrificial action, the one who instituted it so that the liturgy we accomplish with faith may have the gift of the presence of your Son in the hidden sublimity of your sacrament.

C. *Anglican*

Church of England The Order for Holy Communion Rite A (between the Sanctus and the institution, and after the anamnesis:)

Accept our praises, heavenly Father, through your Son, our Saviour Jesus Christ; and as we follow his example and obey his command, grant that by the power of your Holy Spirit these gifts of bread and wine may be to us his body and his blood . . .
. . . and as we eat and drink these holy gifts in the presence of your divine majesty, renew us by your Spirit, inspire us with your love, and unite us in the body of your Son, Jesus Christ our Lord.

Episcopal Church of the USA 1971 (2 Sunday services and 4 occasional services, trial use).

1. (After the anamnesis:)

. . . deign to bless and sanctify, by your Word and your Holy Spirit these gifts of bread and of wine, that, receiving them accord-

ing to the holy institution of your Son our Saviour Jesus Christ, we may be sharers in his most holy Body and his Blood.

2. (After the anamnesis:)

We celebrate the memorial of our redemption, O Father, in this sacrifice of praise and thanksgiving, and we offer these gifts to you.

Sanctify them by your Spirit, that they may be for your people the Body and the Blood of your Son, the holy food and drink of the new and eternal life in him.

Sanctify us also that we may receive this holy Sacrament with faith, that we may serve you in unity, perseverance and peace; and at the last day, bring us with all the saints into the joy of your eternal Kingdom.

a. (After the institution:)

Remembering his death and resurrection, we offer in thanksgiving this bread and this cup.

And we pray you to send your Holy Spirit upon this oblation and upon your people, to transform us and to unite us in your Kingdom.

b. (After the anamnesis:)

. . . we ask you, Father, through the power of the Holy Spirit, to accept these gifts and to bless them. Make us one with your Son in his sacrifice, that his life may be renewed in us.

c. (Between the Sanctus and the institution:)

Father, we who have been redeemed by him and made a new people by water and the Spirit, bring before you these gifts. Sanctify them by your Holy Spirit that they may be for us the Body and the Blood of Jesus Christ our Saviour. On the night when he was delivered up . . .

d. (Between the Sanctus and the institution:)

Father, we bring to you these gifts. Sanctify them by your Holy Spirit, that they may be for your people the Body and the Blood of Jesus Christ our Lord. On the night in which he was delivered up . . .

D. *Lutheran*

Lutheran Church of Sweden

(It is interesting to compare the edition of 1942 and the three variants of 1976, certainly influenced by the ecumenical agreements.)

1942 (between the post-sanctus and the institution:)

Send your Spirit into our hearts, that he may kindle within us a living faith, and prepare us to celebrate fittingly the memorial of our Saviour and to welcome him when he offers himself to us in his Eucharist.

1976 A (between the post-sanctus and the institution, and after the anamnesis:)

Send your Spirit into our hearts, that he may kindle within us a living faith. Sanctify also by your Spirit this bread and this wine, fruits of the earth and of the labour of men, which we present to you, so that we may share through them in the true body and blood of our Lord Jesus Christ.
Let your Holy Spirit unite us in one body and transform us into a living sacrifice in Christ. Through him, with him, in him . . .

1976 B (idem)

Let your Spirit touch our hearts together with our offerings of bread and of wine that through them we may share in the body and in the blood of Christ . . .
Let us be gathered by the Holy Spirit into one body in Him, that we may witness to his life in the world.

1976 C (between the post-sanctus and the institution:)

Shed your Spirit upon us and upon these offerings so that we share in the eternal bread and in the cup of blessing which are the body and the blood of Christ . . .

Lutheran Churches of the USA, 1978 (after the anamnesis:)

Send now, we pray, your Holy Spirit, the spirit of our Lord and of his resurrection, that we who receive the Lord's body and blood may live to the praise of your glory and receive our inheritance with all your saints in light.

Evangelical Lutheran Church of France

(It is interesting to compare the edition of 1966 and the ten variants proposed in 1977, certainly influenced by the ecumenical agreements).

1966 (between the Sanctus and the institution:)

Send your Holy Spirit upon us, your chosen people, and infuse with his power your whole Church. May this Spirit of life make from these earthly foods, which you have given us, food for our spirits. That so, in this bread and in this wine, we may have communion in the body and the blood of our Saviour, who, on the night in which he was betrayed . . .

1977 variant II (text of Taizé; between the Sanctus and the institution:)

Lord, God of all the worlds, you are holy and great in your glory. Send your Holy Spirit upon us and our Eucharist. Consecrate this bread to be the body of Christ, and this cup to be the blood of Christ. May the Holy Spirit, Creator, accomplish the word of your beloved Son, who, on the night in which he was delivered up . . .

1977 variant III (between the Sanctus and the institution:)

Lord, send upon us and upon these offerings your Holy Spirit, that this bread and this wine may give us communion in the body and the blood of your Son.

1977 variant VIII (adaptation of the liturgy of St James; between the Sanctus and the institution)

Lord, send upon us and upon these gifts your Holy Spirit of life, who reigns with you, Father, and your only Son. He spoke under the Law and by the Prophets. He came down upon our Lord at the Jordan, and upon the holy apostles on the day of the first Pentecost. Send this same Spirit that his coming may sanctify this bread and make of it the body of Christ, this cup and make it the blood of Christ.

E. *Reformed* (Calvinist tradition)

Church of Scotland, edition of 1962. (After the post-sanctus and before the institution, which, in this liturgy, comes at the end of the eucharistic prayer)

Wherefore, having in remembrance the work and passion of our Saviour Christ, and pleading His eternal sacrifice, we Thy servants do set forth this memorial, which He hath commanded us to make; and we most humbly beseech Thee to send down Thy Holy Spirit to sanctify both us and these Thine own gifts of bread and wine which we set before Thee, that the bread which we break may be the Communion of the body of Christ, and the cup of blessing which we bless the Communion of the blood of Christ; that we, receiving them, may by faith be made partakers of His body and blood, with all His benefits, to our spiritual nourishment and growth in grace, and to the glory of Thy most holy name.

Reformed Church of France, three texts from the revision of 1976 (after the anamnesis)

1. *Send upon us your Holy Spirit, that, receiving this bread and this cup, we may be granted communion in the body and in the blood of your Son.*

76

2. *Send upon us your Holy Spirit, that, through this bread and this wine, his presence may be given to us.*

3. *Humbly we ask you for your Holy Spirit; that he may grant us to share in the body and in the blood of Christ and gather us into one body. We implore your kindness upon us all: grant that with the witnesses of your people, with Peter, Paul and the other Apostles, Mary and the faithful of all ages, we may share in eternal life and sing your praise, through Jesus Christ, your beloved Son. Through him, with him and in him . . .*

Conclusion

Great progress has been made on both sides since the Second Vatican Council, whether on the level of theological rapprochement, or on that of concrete relationships between Churches. The Roman Catholic Church has desired to apply in the best way possible the principles of the conciliar texts, in particular the Decree on ecumenism *Unitatis Redintegratio*.

In this way a profound communion in the conception and the role of the Word of God in the heart of the Church has developed substantially, on the basis of the results of the ecumenical conference on Faith and Order, at Montreal, in 1963, and the conciliary Constitution, *Dei Verbum*.

Unity in one single Christian baptism was strongly evinced by the Council, particularly under the influence of Cardinal Bea, and made the subject of a close study by the Faith and Order department of the World Council of Churches, in which theologians of all Christian communions, including Roman Catholic theologians, are at work. These combined findings allow the Churches to recognize their baptism mutually and so to affirm that all Christians are visibly united by one and the same sacrament which incorporates them into the Body of Christ.

One important text of the conciliar Decree *Unitatis Redintegratio* had few repercussions after the Council; it concerns the celebration of the Lord's Supper in the Churches born of the Reformation: 'although they do not enjoy that full unity with us of which baptism is the source, and although we believe that, especially owing to the absence of the sacrament of ordination, they have not preserved the characteristic and integral substance of the eucharistic mystery, the ecclesial communities separated from us, however, profess, when they celebrate in the Lord's Supper the memorial of the death and resurrection of the Lord, that life consists in communion with Christ and that they await his glorious return.' (UR, No. 22)

In the light of the conciliar text, the Catholic Church affirms:

1. Our common baptism should lead us on to *the eucharistic life*;
2. The Churches born of the Reformation have not kept *the sacrament of ordination*: a '*defectus*' in them;
3. and so they have not kept *all the reality proper* to the eucharistic mystery;
4. however, they do celebrate at the Lord's Supper *the memorial* of the death and the resurrection of the Lord;
5. they profess that life consists in *communion with Christ*;
6. they await *the return* of Christ in glory.

The Council has recognized that 'many sacred acts of the Christian religion are accomplished among the separated brethren. . . Certainly they are able to produce effectively the life of grace, and it must be recognized that they open the door to the communion of salvation' (UR, No. 3). Cardinal Bea has commented: 'The decree, it is true, does not specify which are these sacred acts. But how could we conceive that among them is not precisely that one which is at the centre of Christian worship (the Lord's Supper)? (Eucharistic Congress at Pisa, June 10 1965, *Documentation catholique*, September 5, 1965, col. 1476).

These positive elements ought to allow the Catholic Church to attach a real value to the Eucharist celebrated by the Churches born of the Reformation and to encourage these Churches in practice ever more frequent, ever more faithful to their own tradition as it reflects the tradition received from the apostles. The deepening of eucharistic doctrine and the development of the eucharistic life in each Church are the surest way of one day finding visible unity around the same Table.

True ecumenism develops best when we recognize all the gifts that the Holy Spirit has given and continues to give to our still separated brethren. It is in this sense that Cardinal Bea was able to say: 'It is not for us to scrutinize the mysteries of divine

Providence and his merciful ways of helping and vitalizing those who, sincerely, serve him with their best. All we have said is enough to affirm that, equally for our non-Catholic brothers of the Reformation, the Lord's Supper can be and is a source of unifying grace, although in the manner and the measure known to God alone. This, then, is true that in quite general terms for all Christians, the more they unite with Christ in eating his Body and drinking his Blood, the more we will arrive progressively at overcoming present divisions and realizing that full unity to which all are called in virtue of baptism.' (*op. cit.*, col. 1477.)

Works in which the epicleses quoted may be found:

Prex eucharistica, textes des liturgies anciennes, Ed. Universitaires, Fribourg, 1968.

Hippolyte de Rome, *La tradition apostolique*, coll. 'Sources chrétiennes.' Le Cerf, Paris.

A. HAMMAN, *Prières des premiers chrétiens*, Fayard, Paris, 1955. *La Messe, liturgies anciennes*, Grasset, Paris, 1964.

Missel Romain, Éd. Jounel, Desclée, Paris, 1971.

Messale Ambrosiano, Milan, 1976.

An Order for Holy Communion, Central Board of Finance of the Church of England (Anglican)

Services for trial use, Church Hymnal Corporation, New York, 1971 (Episcopal)

Lutherische Agende I, Lutherisches Verlagshaus, Berlin, 1962

Service Book and Hymnal, Augsburg Publishing House, Minneapolis, 1961 (Lutheran)

Liturgie I et II, Église évangélique luthérienne de France, Paris, 1966; see also the liturgical texts for trial use. 1977 (16, rue Chauchat, Paris 9ᵉ).

The Book of Common Order, Church of Scotland, Oxford University Press, London, 1962

Liturgie, Église Réformée de France, Berger-Levrault, Paris, 1963

Information-Évangélisation, n° 3, 47 rue de Clichy, Paris, 1976